Praise for this book

"Reading this book has been a great learning experience for me. Every person in the world, young or old, male or female, needs the teachings given in this book. This is the book of life, the book of foundation, the foundation of life. It must reach every university, every school, every market association, every government department and every club like Rotary and Lion's.

This book will teach the young generation, which is our country's future, how the foundation of life is built. This book is a revolution in itself! When this revolution gathers momentum, our nation shall be recreated. The whole world needs this book. The world can change on the foundation of this book."

— **Dr. Kiran Bedi**
First Indian woman IPS Officer
First woman police commissioner
Ramon Magsaysay Award winner

"I work in the field of education. Do you know what kind of knowledge has the power to change our inner state of being and transform our character? This book of Sirshree is one such book that can change our character into a formidable one. The teachings, spiritual discourses and many of the books of Sirshree have the power to completely transform a human being."

— **Dr. Vijay Bhatkar**
Inventor of India's first supercomputer 'Param 8000'
Padmashree Award winner for Supercomputing
Dataquest Lifetime Achievement Award winner

Also by Sirshree

Spiritual Masterpieces - Self Realisation books for serious seekers

The Secret of Awakening
The Source of Silence : Journey Inward to the True Self
100% Karma: Learn the Art of Conscious Karma that Liberates
100% Meditation: Dip into the Stillness of Pure Awareness
You are Meditation: Discover Peace and Bliss Within
Essence of Devotion: From Devotee to Divinity
The Supreme Quest: Your search for the Truth ends there where you are
Secret of The Third Side of The Coin
Seek Forgiveness & be Free: Liberation from Karmic Bondage
Passworads to a Happy Life: The Art of Being Happy in all Situations

Self Help Treasures - Self Development books for success seekers

The Source of Health: The Key to Perfect Health Discovery
Inner Ninety Hidden Infinity: How to build your book of values
Inner 90 for Youth: The secret of reaching and staying at the peak of success
The Source for Youth: You have the power to change your life
Inner Magic: The Power of self-talk
The Power of Present: Experience the Joy of the Now
You are Not Lazy: A story of shifting from Laziness to Success
Freedom From Fear, Worry, Anger: How to be cool, calm and courageous
The Little Gita of Problem Solving: Gift of 18 Solutions to Any Problem

New Age Nuggets - Practical books on applied spirituality and self help

The Source: Power of Happy Thoughts
Secret of Happiness: Instant Happiness - Here and Novw!
Help God to Help You: Whatever you do, do it with a smile
Ultimate Purpose of Success: Achieving Success in all five aspects of life
Celebrating Relationships: Bringing Love, Life, Laughter in Your Relations
Everything is a Game of Beliefs: Understanding is the Whole Thing
Detachment From Attachment: Gift of Freedom From Suffering
Emotional Freedom Through Spiritual Wisdom

Profound Parables - Fiction books containing profound truths

Beyond Life: Conversations on Life After Death
The One Above: What if God was your neighbour?
The Warrior's Mirror: The Path To Peace
Master of Siddhartha: Revealing the Truth of Life and After-life
Put Stress to Rest: Utilizing Stress to Make Progress
The Source @ Work: A Story of Inspiration from Jeeodee

Inner Ninety
Hidden Infinity

How to build your book of values

The secret of staying at the peak of success

Inner Ninety, Hidden Infinity
By **Sirshree** Tejparkhi

Copyright © Tejgyan Global Foundation
All Rights Reserved 2008

Tejgyan Global Foundation is a charitable organization
with its headquarters in Pune, India.

ISBN : 978-81-8415-307-1

Published by WOW Publishings Pvt. Ltd., India

First edition: March 2008

Sixth edition: April 2022

Printed and bound by Trinity Academy, Pune, INDIA

This book is the translation of the Hindi book titled
"Neev Ninety - Naitik Mulyonki Sampatti" by Sirshree Tejparkhi.

Copyrights are reserved with Tejgyan Global Foundation and publishing rights are vested exclusively with WOW Publishings Pvt. Ltd. This book is sold subject to the condition that it shall not by way of trade or otherwise, be lent, resold, hired out, or otherwise circulated without the publisher's prior written consent in any form of binding or cover other than that in which it is published and without a similar condition including this condition being imposed on the subsequent purchaser and without limiting the rights under copyright reserved above, no part of this publication may be reproduced, stored in or introduced into a retrieval system, or transmitted, in any form, or by any means, electronic, mechanical, photocopying, recording or otherwise, without the prior written permission of both the copyright owner and the above-mentioned publisher of this book. Any person who does any unauthorized act in relation to this publication may be liable to criminal prosecution and civil claims for damages.

Although the author and publisher have made every effort to ensure accuracy of content in this book, they hereby disclaim any liability to any party for any loss, damage, or disruption caused by errors or omissions, resulting from negligence, accident, or any other cause. Readers are advised to take full responsibility to exercise discretion in understanding and applying the content of this book.

To,
The world's greatest books
and their authors, editors, proof-readers,
assistants, typeset designers,
graphic designers and printing-press workers.

These books are:
Bhagawad Gita, Koran, Bible,
Dhammapada, Guru Granth Sahib,
Yog Vasishtha, Bhagawad Puran, Dnyaneshwari,
Dasbodh, Sri Ramcharitmanas, Mahabharata

Table of Contents

Three Divisions of An Undivided Book

PART I	**Foundation 90**	**11**
Day 1	**Hundred Ninety Ten Zero** Foundation90 + Top10 + Hidden0 = Blessing of a Complete Character	13
Day 2	**What Kind Of A Book Are You** How to be the best person	18
Day 3	**Why is Training of Foundation 90 Necessary** Beware of character degradation	27
Day 4	**Eight Causes That Weaken Foundation90** Engage in healthy contemplation	31
Day 5	**Eight Consequences of a Weak Foundation90** An unsuccessful life is such	41
Day 6	**Acquire the Quality of Enhancing the Primary Ten Qualities** Secret of knowing and appreciating qualities First remedy	46
Day 7	**Self-introspect** Remove the weakness of not being able to listen about your weaknesses Second remedy	50
Day 8	**Let Your Aim be the Pilot of Your Life** Make the right choice between aim and gain Third remedy	54
Day 9	**Bright Untruth and Dark Lies** Learn from every mistake Fourth remedy	60

Day 10	**Beware of Unhealthy Entertainment**	
	Employ 10 steps for healthy entertainment	
	Fifth remedy	65
Day 11	**Choose the Right Friends**	
	Don't sit under a toddy palm tree	
	Sixth remedy	70
Day 12	**Enhance Your Maturity**	
	Become a complete person	
	Seventh remedy	76
Day 13	**Enhance Your Mental Maturity**	
	Make your mind loving, pure and unshakeable	
	Eighth remedy	81
Day 14	**Become Trustworthy**	
	Reinforce your four strengths	
	Ninth remedy	85
Day 15	**Improve Yourself**	
	Handwriting and Reading Autobiographies	
	Tenth remedy	94
Day 16	**Four Steps to Fortify Your Foundation90**	
	How to transform your negative energy	
	Eleventh remedy	97
Day 17	**Contemplate on Religious Texts**	
	Different texts, One message	
	Twelfth remedy – Delving into contemplation	102
Day 18	**Contemplate on the Teachings of Saints**	
	Several Saints, One message	
	Thirteenth remedy – Contemplation statement	106
Part II	**Top10**	**113**
Day 19	**Do Not Consider Top10 to be Everything**	
	Beware of cheap publicity	115
Day 20	**Do Not Misuse Your Top10**	
	Unimpressive Top10 is also a grace	120

Day 21	Develop Maturity of Your Top10	
	Let your body language give out only one signal	124
Part III	**Hidden Infinity or Hidden Zero**	**129**
Day 22	Living in Zero is the Reality	
	90+10+0 = 100%	131
Day 23	Zero Experience is Beyond Inside and Outside	
	Free Sample	134
Day 24	Two Aspects of Understanding Zero	
	The Self Experience Truth	138
Day 25	Enhance Your Spiritual Maturity	
	Maturity in Inner Silence	144
	Blessing of a Good Character	**151**
Day 26	Epitome of Self-Development	
	Mahatma Gandhi	153
Day 27	A Unique Combination of Love, Affection, Sacrifice and Service	
	Mother Teresa	158
Day 28	Symbol of Knowledge, Inspiration and Great Deeds	
	Swami Vivekananda	162
Day 29	Ocean of Detachment, Devotion, Service and Forgiveness	
	Saint Tukaram	167
Day 30	Let Your Guru Shape Your Foundation	
	Recognise the tools of the Guru - Final remedy	173
	Appendices	**177**

How to get the maximum from this book

By reading this book every denizen of this world can become a master of the wealth of character. To get the maximum from this book, you can read the suggestions given below:

1. The chapters in this book have been named as 'days'. This is because this book is a kind of self-course where you can read a chapter a day for a month and imbibe the teachings in your life step by step so as to gain a strong and firm foundation, i.e. a good and powerful character.

2. To understand the meaning of Inner Ninety (Foundation90 or character) and Top10 (external appearance) in detail and to know the necessity of its training, read Day 1 and Day 3.

3. Day 2 titled 'What kind of book are you?' epitomises man as a book, reading which will enable you to choose the best way of leading your life.

4. To know about the reasons of a weak Foundation90 and its ill-effects, read Day 4 and Day 5.

5. To learn the methods of strengthening your Foundation90, you can read the chapters through Day 6 to Day 18.

6. Readers interested in enhancing their mental, intellectual, physical and spiritual maturity should read Day 12, Day 13, Day 21 and Day 25.

7. To gain the trust of others and become dependable, read Day 14.

8. To wipe out the notion that Top10 is everything, read Part II, Days 19 to 21.

9. To experience the Hidden Infinity and to know its significance, read Part III, Days 22 to 24.

10. To draw inspiration from the character and teachings of some great personalities of the world, read Days 26 to 29.

11. To contemplate over the teachings of holy books and saints, read Days 17 and 18.

Hundred Ninety Ten Zero

Foundation90 + Top10 + Hidden0 = Blessing of a Complete Character

Dear Books,

Man is a book. Understand this through this book. Read this book and strengthen your Inner Ninety. Inner Ninety signifies a person's character. And character is the foundation of an individual, which comprises 90% of his being. Hence Inner Ninety has been referred to as Foundation90.

Top10 stands for the external appearance of the individual, which comprises 10% of his being. If your Foundation90 is already strong, then you can be instrumental for others to strengthen theirs so that happiness, peace and knowledge can spread in this world.

A successful farmer reaps rich harvest because he cultivates those trees whose roots go deep into the soil. He never cultivates trees that will yield only thorns. A successful farmer knows that only the tree whose roots reach deep into the soil becomes a huge strong tree, which bears good fruit and provides cool shade. The roots of the tree symbolise Foundation90. Deeper and stronger the Foundation90, bigger and stronger will be the tree. Trees that have a weak Foundation90 are uprooted even by minor storms.

Man is also a walking talking tree and book. His Foundation90 is his character. If man's character is pure and steadfast, he is able to experience the real happiness of a successful life. The man, whose character is slippery and impure, is driven by false pleasures and in the true sense leads an unsuccessful life. If his character is such that it falters in every little incident or every scene that he comes across, you can rest assured that he is unknowingly sawing the same branch he is sitting on. With the help of good people, even if such a person achieves success, his success will not last long.

In order to understand such an important and profound subject like Foundation90, try comparing man to a book. A book comprises of the cover which has 10% of the information, and the pages inside which hold 90% of the information. Similarly, man's character is made up of his external appearance (10%) and inner faculty (90%). Complete development of character is very essential.

Development of character is possible at any age. Character can be remodelled even in older age. But in that stage, tendencies are seen to have hardened up. In spite of that, you can take up the task of creating a new character by developing the good qualities hidden inside you. For creation of a new character, ask yourself, 'What do people see when they look at me? What are they reminded of when they look at my Top10 [external appearance]? Looking at me, should the thirst for the supreme truth or the attraction for maya [sensory attractions] increase? Which feelings should be evoked in them looking at my external appearance?' When people look at our external appearance i.e. Top10, they should be able to see how an 'ideal life' should be. That is why, we have to check our Foundation90 so that we can do its proof-reading (remove its flaws). We should be able to eliminate whatever is unnecessary from our Top10 and decide on what should be written on which page of our book. Whatever is printed inside our book is our Foundation90.

When your Foundation90 becomes strong, the remaining 10% (Top10) will automatically appear good to people. How do you look at Mahatma Gandhi or Mother Teresa today? As soon as you hear their names, you go beyond their body, straight to their roots. You appreciate their qualities and integrity. You can only see the 'wisdom of life' that has assimilated inside them. The 'wisdom of life' is obtained by going through the bitter-sweet experiences of life. This wisdom is printed beautifully in every virtuous person. Their external appearance comprises only 10%. You do not stop at their body or book cover. You do not stop at the external appearance of great devotees such as Sudama or Shabari, because you immediately begin to see what is printed inside, what is hidden inside (their moral fibre and Experience of Being). This is man's real wealth and treasure, which he must zealously guard, maintain and enhance.

It is only man's integrity that earns him people's trust. People should be able to come and tell you, 'We have faith in you. You always do what you say, what you say is what you think, and what you think is what you feel. That means, your feelings, thoughts, words and actions are unidirectional and in complete harmony.' This will begin to happen with you when people read you, know you and understand you closely. Else people often look only at our cover (body) and make assumptions about us. That is the reason we waste all our precious time in beautifying our body. Notwithstanding that the contents printed inside the book account for ninety percent. This is the foundation – 90% – which is the secret of achieving real success and staying there at the top.

Today's young generation should be taught about Foundation90 in schools and colleges because you can see youths today throwing away the wealth of character at the roadsides. They observe film stars in movies and on television and are swept away by the glitz, glamour and their dreamlike but illusory lifestyle. They do not understand that the lifestyle of actors is only their profession. It is only for money that we are taken on a joy-ride into the dream-world. There is no foundation to these dreams. Castles in the air are just beautiful illusions. That is why young people should first be taught how to make their Foundation90 strong and sturdy.

Only those people whose foundation is sound should guide the upcoming generation, because only such people can show them the right direction. Those, who have a weak foundation and are completely unaware of the importance of a good firm character, never even get the thought that they should tell others something that can help them to build up their character.

The responsibility of guiding the next generation should be taken up by people reading this book. All around you, you can see the aimless young generation roaming around. Motivate them to read good books and listen to the Truth message so that they can develop their inner strength and become strong and virtuous. The young generation is the future of our world, hence they need to be given the right guidance at the right time. These young ones will then develop a complete and powerful character and thank you for it.

Complete character (HundredNinetyTenZero) is formed by Foundation90 + Top10 + Hidden Zero. Hidden Zero is the hidden God or Hidden Infinity inside man, which has been given many different names by different religions, nations and cultures. Every job is incomplete without the Infinity or Zero. With the help of the Hidden Infinity, man can reach the highest peak of life and experience fulfilment and eternal bliss. By spreading this fragrance of bliss and contentment among the people around him, he can set up an example.

Such a person takes up the responsibility of fortifying the foundation of society so that a healthy, vice-free society can be formed and the entire human race can attain Mission Earth. Mission Earth or the purpose for which man is born on Earth is that every human being has to make his mind unshakeable, pure and loving. It is with this mission or objective in mind that this book has been written, which is not only a self-retreat* but can also prove to be your Guru or holy text. So come, follow the instructions of the Guru (of reading this whole book) and make your book of life worthy of reading.

In a self-retreat, you can read one chapter of the book a day and deeply contemplate over the contents of that chapter. In this way, in thirty days, you will become a knower and creator of Foundation90.

DAY 2

What Kind Of A Book Are You

How to be the best person

People are living books; learn to read them. You can learn thousands of ways of leading your lives by reading each person. By reading some individuals, you may learn new and superlative ways of living, and by reading some others you may observe old and beaten unhappy ways of living. Therefore, ask yourself:

- When people read me, what kind of life should they learn to lead? – What is the title that should be printed on my book?
- By reading me, will people be bored or learn a wrong way of living life?
- When people read me today, what kind of life are they learning to lead? And in future, what will I inspire people to learn from my life?

These questions will totally awaken the consciousness inside you. When you decide upon the answers to these questions, your life will get a powerful, well-defined direction.

Is the title of your book 'Bungle in the Jungle'? Some people's books carry the titles 'The Swindler', 'Crooked Ways', 'The Criminal' 'Charlatan', 'Jewel Thief' or 'The Traitor', i.e. their character is shady. You may want to stay away from such people. These titles of books may seem like names of movies to you, but that is not so. Characterless, aimless, conscienceless people involved in crimes, thefts, bungling, gambling and hooliganism are seen roaming the streets in society. Fifty percent of the matter in newspapers and television channels is dedicated to such people. Such people are a curse on the society, nation and the world.

The title of people's books can be 'The Peacekeeper' or even 'Thief of Baghdad'. Through their books, people spread either peace or unrest in society. Some people's books are titled 'Nothing', while some others carry the title 'Dumb and Dumber'. But what title do you want to give to your book?

Reading the matter above, you may be wondering, 'How these names of movies will guide us in the right direction? What do these names have to do with this book?' But as you continue to read this book titled 'Inner Ninety, Hidden Infinity', the reality will soon appear before you.

How is the title of a book coined? The deeds (karma) that you do decide your character or the title of your book. The physical or mental actions done by a person all through the day, which have an effect on him or his surroundings, are called karma. This means that the feelings, thoughts, words and actions of man are all karma because all these factors affect him and his surroundings. The result of your karma decides what will be the title of your book. If the results of man's karma produce ill-effects, the title of his book will be something like 'Don', 'The Villain' or 'The Con'. If the results of man's karma produce good and powerful effects, his book may be titled along the lines of 'The Loyal 47', 'The Patriot' 'Mr. India', 'Arjun', 'The Good Samaritan' or 'Krishna'.

The manner in which a person leads his life can decide the title of his book. The one who lives like 'Alibaba' or 'Aladdin' will have the title 'Forty Thieves' or 'Magic Lamp' on his book. These titles give man an aim, the direction of which can be either right or wrong.

The name of a book should divulge its contents and the contents or subject matter should determine the name of the book. Some book may have mystery as the subject matter while some other may have devotion and hymns as the subject matter. So the names of these books could be 'Harry Potter' or 'The Devotee Prahlad'.

In this chapter you are being suggested several names, based on which you can decide on the title of your book, i.e. in one word you can enunciate your character. If some book is titled 'Meerabai' or 'Muktabai', what do you see their character as – virtuous or characterless? The answer is clear. 'Meerabai' and 'Muktabai' are the favourite books in the school of divine devotion. Be it 'Meerabai' or 'Munnabhai', if every name spells out man's aim, then there is importance of names; else what is in the name? If the name of the book is able to give man his purpose of life, then the name can mean everything.

Some people's book of life can even be titled as 'Spiderman', 'Hanuman', 'Superman', 'Master of Destiny' or 'Messengers of Love'. This means all these people want to destroy the dazzling but corrupt world of demons and villains with their divine service and power and lead this world to peace and well-being.

People who are always lost in the past have the title of their books as 'Nostalgia', 'Lost in Thoughts', 'Nowhere to go' 'Stuck in the Past', etc. Such people live far, far away from the present and the reality.

Those who wish to live in the present will say, 'Tomorrow never comes'. If your book carries the name 'Today's Arjun', how will you like to be guided? What questions will you ask Lord Krishna is what this book's title enunciates.

The one living in the future has the title of his book as 'Back to the Future', 'Castles in the Air', 'Daydreamer', 'Daydream Obsession', 'Daydream Believer' or 'The Procrastinator'. Such people build castles in the air but forget to build their foundations. What should ideally happen is that one should pull away from the past and future and make their Foundation90 strong in the present.

The person who thinks that life is a burden may have the title of 'The Porter' and the one who lives considering life to be God's divine play may have the title 'Maha-Aasmani' (Supreme Truth directly from the heavens).

The title of man's book of life will be according to the way he takes his life to be. If you want to create a No. 1 book, decide on your subject matter. You have to choose your own subject.

'How to become a best Doctor ' can also be the name of a book. If you are studying medicine, you will want to create such a book so that you can become a source of inspiration for many doctors to come.

Your book can be titled as 'Ways to become the best teacher', 'How to become the best devotee', 'How to become a good businessman', 'How to become a truthful lawyer' and so forth. In this way there can be many different titles according to their different objectives.

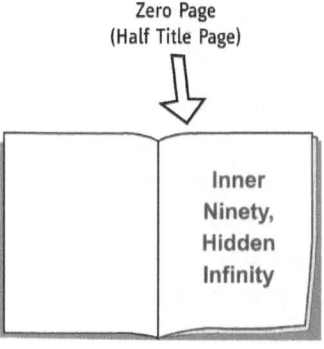

Books also have a subtitle. Many a time you carry out two roles, hence you can also give a subtitle. In addition, you can insert a highlighter and state the important points in a more impressive way. You decide what you want. What should the title be on the front page of your book? The title of the book should match the contents given inside.

Sometimes there are some books that don't even have a cover, but prove to be excellent books. You often come across such books in old stacks of a used-books store. You might stumble onto some extraordinary wealth of knowledge in these books. Maybe these books have lessons on 'The Art of Thinking' or 'The Art of Learning'. Many people are not even aware that thinking and learning are an art, which are worthy of learning. How to learn and how to achieve excellence in a particular field are what we need to learn – be it learning how to cycle or how to learn a new language. Some books may prove to be brilliant in spite of a torn cover. Hence do not go by the cover of a book (i.e., the Top 10).

You know that every book has only one table of contents. A book should never have two tables of contents. The whole book ought to be neatly arranged and written according to one table of contents only.

The table of contents of our book ought to show how our life can be instrumental for others. In some books like 'True Lies', there are two tables of contents. One is just for showing and the other is the reality. What is written in the table of contents is not what is there inside the book. Everything is a bungle. Like an elephant's teeth, the real table of contents is hidden. Such books claim to be full of mystery and adventure, but are actually not even suitable for trash.

Can you assertively proclaim today: 'I am going to live my life in this particular manner. Even through difficult times, I am going to live according to the principles I have set for myself. I am going to follow these set of rules and regulations. Then whatever happens, let any kind of difficulties crop up, I am not going to budge from these principles. I will stay away from those things that can degrade my character. If consuming alcohol deteriorates my character, I will never touch it.' In this way decide for yourself and fearlessly declare: 'These are my life's principles and I will always abide by them. To guard my integrity, I will never fall prey to any addictions.'

Man becomes a slave to addictions because he does not determine the principles of his life. Initially man consumes substances of addiction and then addictions consume him.

A person was taking his dog for a walk. He came across a drunkard along the way. The drunkard asked him, 'You are walking along with your dog. Can you tell me what is the difference between a dog and man?' The person replied, 'A dog may drink any amount of alcohol but cannot become a man. But by drinking just two pegs, man can become any kind of animal.'

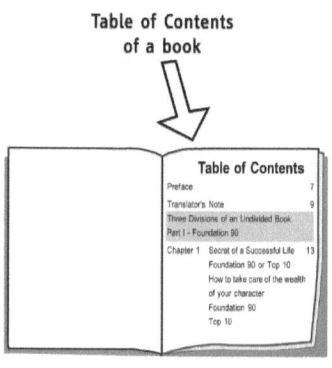

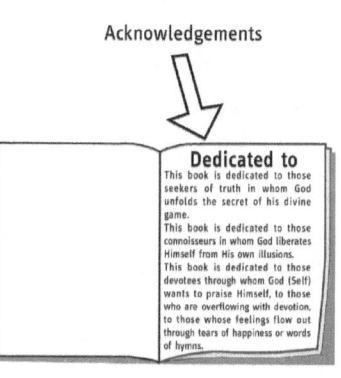

A father reprimanded his son saying, 'Are you a donkey to chew tobacco? Tobacco is like grass and donkeys chew grass.' The son retorted, 'I am not a donkey; I am a tiger.' His father remarked, 'Donkey or tiger, after all you are an animal!'

Since we are born as humans, i.e. we have received the cover of this human body, we must live like humans and not like animals. We need to establish some principles in our life and stay firm on them. There shouldn't be two tables of contents in our book; there must be only one table of contents according to which we must move ahead.

People who want to fulfil their selfish desires make two tables of contents. Such people live one kind of life to show others and another kind of life in secrecy doing some illicit activities. Since they have two tables of contents, they always live in uncertainty, thinking, 'What should I say to this person and what should I tell that person? Will I be caught red-handed? Yesterday I gave this person some wrong information and I had lied to that person, will he question me?' This way such people live in constant anxiety. Those who have only one table of contents have no such worries.

When you open a book, the first thing you see on page one is the title. On the next page there are acknowledgements, in which you read 'thanks or gratitude to… ' or 'this book is dedicated to…' In your book of life too, thank those people who are aiding you in your progress. Whatever you give thanks for, blossoms and enhances in your life. Your book of life has to blossom and open up too; else it will be left unread and closed like many others.

Your book's preface or prologue is your statement of life. What is the 'mission statement' of your life? A preface describes in short the contents of the entire book. State in short what your life is all about and what are the prospects of your life that your preface spells out.

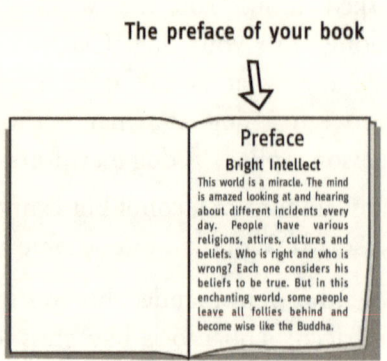

Some person gives his 'mission statement' as: *In two years' time I will start living a life beyond two, i.e. beyond duality.* Thus he related his mission statement in a few words. Here 'statement' means the principles you have set for your life, your definition of life, what you consider your life to be, your understanding of life.

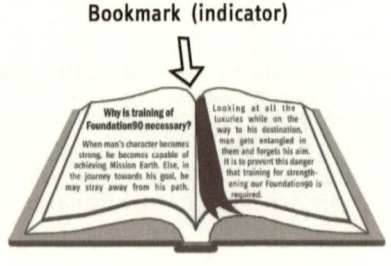

Every person should prepare his mission statement like, 'This is my prologue: I am going to live life openly, to its fullest, in full bloom. My life will speak for itself.' Someone's prologue could be: 'Whoever I meet should go back a better person, or at least remain as he was earlier. After meeting me, nobody should leave in a worse condition than before, i.e. nobody's level of consciousness should fall on meeting me.' In this way, if life's principles are decided beforehand, you find it easier to deal with various situations of life. Like if someone offers you a drink and says, 'Come on, try it!', you know clearly what to accept and what not to, due to your prologue. You will very easily and confidently say that 'this is not in my calling...' Then the opposite person does not force you much. If you haven't decided your principles, then even a slight hesitation on your part conveys to the other person that if you are pushed a little more, you are going to accept the offer. This happens because there is no preface (principles) at all in your book. There are many books in which the preface is totally missing.

Many people do not read the preface of a book. Always read the preface. There is something important written in it, like, how to read the book, which aspects you need to look into and contemplate, especially where to give more attention, etc. In your preface too, write some pointers so that when people meet you, they learn exactly what you want them to learn from you.

Some books have bookmarks so that one can stop for a while, think and contemplate. To continually benefit from a book, bookmarks play an important role. Bookmarks remind us till where we have learnt the last time around, so that further things can be learnt without any delay. Are you able to give the right reminders to people so that they awaken? Do you remember the things you had inspired in people the last time you met them? When you take interest in people, you are able to work as a bookmark or indicator in the right manner.

A book becomes complete when the preface, half-title page, table of contents, text and everything is done. The book is divided into parts; not for confusion but for convenience. Different chapters are made so that the book is easy to understand. After reading the book you realise that the book was an undivided whole. The book, in which feelings, thoughts, words and actions are one, has a strong Foundation90.

The person who is the same inside as well as outside will say, 'My life is an open book; anybody can read it. I am the same inside and out.' Only such a person is able to make his character pure, because his Foundation90 is unyielding and he has gained the trust of others.

A book in which all the chapters are scattered around and disorganised causes confusion instead of providing solutions. Such a book is a hypocrite. Therefore, ask yourself the question, 'Do I practise what I preach? Do my feelings and thoughts move in the same direction? Do my words express the same feelings that I actually experience?' If the answer to all these questions is 'yes', then you are an undivided and integrated book. Glad to meet you!

Why is Training of Foundation90 Necessary

Beware of character degradation

Nobody is born with a good or bad character, but you can die with a good or bad character. Every child has a pure, unblemished character, which can get contaminated due to improper upbringing.

Character is like a burning torch. Its sacred radiance inspires many. Just like a building's strength is gauged by its foundation, similarly a person is judged and commended by his character.

The sphere of influence of character is very expansive. It is character that sows the seeds of its qualities deep inside man. When the time arrives, these qualities develop, and create the personality of man. If the seeds of character are healthy, Foundation90 of the person is strong and sturdy. Conversely, if the seeds are infected and weak, man becomes a slave of a feeble character.

Character is the measure by which man is recognised and understood. Character is not made up of external appearance and adornments, but of qualities, knowledge and selfdiscipline. Trustworthiness, constant thirst for achieving the goal, and purity of mind help in bolstering the Foundation90. Learn to take advantage of these aids.

People have fostered several different notions about character. 'Character ' is supposed to be only regarding relations between a man and a woman. Character has thus been relegated inside a small sphere. If a person behaves well externally in man-woman relationships but is filled with thoughts of sensual enjoyments, people still think of him to have a virtuous character. This is utterly wrong. Such relationships are merely one aspect of character. Thus, everyone should here understand that 'character' should prove to be true in the litmus test of all qualities.

When man's character becomes strong, he becomes capable of achieving Mission Earth. Else, in his journey towards his aim, he may get stuck at various eye-catching sites. He may indulge in the comforts, pleasures and lavish amenities that come his way, and forget his goal. It is to prevent this danger from happening that the training of strengthening Foundation90 is crucial. Try to understand through the following story, when and how moral values are useful in man's life.

A person sets out in the journey towards the Supreme Truth. On the way he comes across a town where he meets many movie characters. He finds those movie stars and their looks to be very alluring, so he thinks that staying in this town is a better idea. He puts his aim at stake for sake of the movie actors, because all those beautiful faces of which he was a great fan and always desired to see in person, were actually present in that town. He thinks to himself, 'All those whom I always wanted to meet are there in this town. All those fascinating faces that I wanted to see can be seen in this town. There is so much joy here; what is the need of continuing my journey any further? I shall stay here.'

In this way, the person is pulled towards those movie characters and their lifestyles, due to which, his character degrades. His Guru already knows where he is going to get stuck in his journey and that is why before the commencement of the journey, the Guru puts him through a sadhana (spiritual practice). In order that he completes his journey uninterrupted and not indulge in such characters, his Foundation90 is worked upon. This training is necessary because in the journey towards the highest goal, man should be able to keep his mind unwavering and pure, and not get caught in worldly attractions and pleasures.

When man sets out on his journey on his vehicle without making his mind unshakeable and pure, he spots a rabbit (distraction) scurrying across his path into the jungle. He halts his vehicle and runs after the rabbit in the jungle. In such a situation, a judicious person would ask himself, 'Is running after the rabbit my need or is it my want?' On getting the answer he would resume his journey, because such rabbits do keep coming all the time. When man contemplates upon his decisions with awareness, he realises his mistake. Then as a virtuous person, and not a characterless one, he leaves behind the eye-catching town and resumes his journey towards the Truth.

Maha Nirvan Nirmaan means the highest creation, the ultimate goal and success of the Universal Self. It can be achieved only after self-realisation and self-stabilisation. In the journey towards Maha Nirvan Nirmaan, such things, such towns (delicacies, amenities, security, status, respect, fame, power) can halt man in the way and entangle him. If he falls for these infatuations and stops his journey towards the Truth, what bigger loss can he suffer! This means, in spite of getting a human birth, the ultimate goal, and guidance to attain it, he does not reach the destination. To achieve your destination and not go astray before you reach the destination, wouldn't you like to fortify your Foundation90? Wouldn't you like to wipe out the eight causes of breakdown of Foundation90? Gather all this knowledge in the next chapter so that never again can a rabbit, greed, attraction or a glitzy town stop you in your journey towards the ultimate goal.

Eight Causes That Weaken Foundation90

Engage in healthy contemplation

To make your aim powerful, reinforcing its foundation is vitally essential. Oftentimes people tend to overlook this need because the foundation is invisible. Foundation needs to be strong for everything, right from building a sturdy house to enhancing your personality. People cannot understand the importance of foundation because it is built using subtle or finer elements. People readily understand grosser things but cannot stay focused on Foundation90, which is made up of subtle elements. That is why the effects of a weak foundation show up quickly.

In ignorance, man's state of mind becomes such that he himself pushes off his life into a dark valley. He complicates his life so much under the influence of ignorance and ego that it becomes difficult for him to come out of it. Many a time he may spend an entire lifetime untangling the knots of his life. To break this tendency of the mind, man should take the help of knowledge. Acquire the knowledge of your ignorance and contemplate vigorously about life. Healthy contemplation will light the torch of awareness in you. With the torch of awareness, you can straighten out your life and thereby keep your Foundation90 strong easily.

Keeping in mind all these aspects, get your character rid of the eight causes given below. These causes may seem ordinary to you but it is only due to the combination of these causes that man's foundation becomes weak.

1. The falsehood of 'two' and life of duality

When man loses the simplicity of his life, and infatuated with greed and desires, cunningly deceives people, he lives a dual life. One life, like an elephant's tusks, is for showing to people and the other life is what he actually leads. By leading two different lives, he becomes a hypocrite. He needs to struggle hard to handle a dual life, due to which he lives in constant physical and mental stress.

Initially man enjoys leading a dual life but very soon he is exposed and he plunges into the depths of failure or becomes a criminal.

The person living a dual life, caught in illusory attractions, harms not only himself but also instigates others knowingly or unknowingly to cheat. Such a person becomes an idol for others to indulge and sink deep into the mire of crime.

The one living a dual life not only commits crimes and harms others, but also ruins his own life. He who deceives himself always lives in falsehood. Due to living in falsehood, his foundation becomes feeble.

2. Greed and lies

Due to greed, man indulges in deceit related to even minor objects and matters, and unnecessarily complicates his life. His avarice forces him to take the refuge of lies. Although there is no need to lie but he thinks, 'What harm will a few lies do? What difference would it make to anyone?'

In reality, everything has been created in abundance for man. Nature has shown man the method to achieve anything he wants. However, in ignorance and under the influence of greed, he thinks, 'If I don't snatch from somebody, I will not get it.' A thief snatches by stealing, political leaders snatch by instigating some incidents, and a common man tries to snatch away things from others by lying. When he does gain something by lying, this habit of his takes root. He becomes untrustworthy and thus puts his character at stake.

In order to augment your character, stop taking help of lies and greed. Even without resorting to greed and lies, you can have everything you want. All you need to do is to read good books, listen to the Truth through discourses, and engage in healthy contemplation. Healthy contemplation implies contemplating maturely, where you are able to tell yourself your own deceit and lies, and talk to yourself honestly.

Man always craves for appreciation. It is for this reason that he develops the habit of lying in order to blow the trumpets of his capabilities in front of one and all. Like, if he took two days to complete a task, he tells people that he worked for ten days on that job. He doesn't tire proclaiming, 'I have put in tremendous efforts and worked tirelessly for days together and only then this job could be accomplished!' He thinks that by speaking this way he is creating a good image among people. And he feels, 'What difference does it make to anybody if I brag and boast this way?' Nobody was harmed by listening to him brag, but the habit of lying definitely took root in him.

If the listener is not aware of the lies, the liar takes unfair advantage of it. By doing so, he not only boosts his habit of lying but also destabilises his own foundation. If such habits are growing in a person, understand that his foundation is weakening. This is a sign of an imminent earthquake in his life. Even mild earthquakes destroy those buildings whose foundations are weak. If such a person does not understand nature's signals, he pays for it by losing his integrity.

Ignorance forces man to lie. Then these lies slowly turn into a habit and become a part of his personality, which he does not even realise. In everyday life he lies several times. Sometimes he is delighted by the success of his lies and tells his friends, 'I lied to that person in this particular manner, and believing me instantly, he did my job. See, what a fool I made of him!'

While narrating his cleverness in this manner, a person has two desires: Firstly, to impress others and earn their praise. He feels high of himself thinking that he can make a fool out of anyone. And secondly, to get his work done without much effort. Both these desires debilitate man's Foundation90.

Some people are plagued with the disease of lying in every little instance. When at home, a person tells his son, 'If someone from my office calls me up, tell him that dad is ill and has gone to see the doctor.' An unemployed youth spends the whole day loitering around with friends and in the evening he comes home and says to his mother, 'I spent the whole day searching for a job but didn't find any. I am tired, I'll take some rest.' In this way, man wants to remain immersed in his unhealthy desires by lying. In his greed for pleasures and comforts, he takes help of lies and nurtures bad habits.

Lying in every small matter is a harmful tendency and man is unabashedly deepening this tendency every day. He does not understand that this tendency is bad karma which will one day reap regretful results.

If someone deceives you or takes you for a ride, you feel pained. Likewise, when you lie, your friends, neighbours and colleagues feel pained too. Hence, if you love your near and dear ones, free yourself from the mesh of greed and lies. As you sow, so you reap. If you wish that your tree has deep roots, stop all those lies which arise out of greed, ignorance and ego.

3. Craving for comforts and luxuries

Those who have a frail Foundation90 always dream of comforts and finishing their jobs without taking any efforts. They not only fear hard work but also want to use shortcuts to success. This very attitude makes their foundation hollow. Such people are always thinking about how to shirk from hard work. Their mind is obsessed with thoughts of how to get rid of their work as early as possible and achieve instant success.

To achieve such success, they can even resort to corruption, malice and taking help of unscrupulous people. How can Foundation90 remain consolidated in the company of bad people?

Those who want to scale the heights of their personal aspirations resort to shortcuts and make their foundation loose and fragile. Such people don't care about their character whatsoever. They are busy mustering money through deceit and fraud and thinking about quickly fulfilling their ambitions. They can go to any lengths to put their life together according to their wishes. Such people can also become a threat to society. The base of these people rests on deceit and fraud.

People having a frail character consider only money to be the means and aim of progress. Their idea of happiness rests on wealth. They preach to others too that they should utilise their skills and talents only to accumulate as much wealth as possible. Looking at them, poor people too develop the desire of making it rich quick. Frustrated with their life, they lose their conscience and turn to wrong ways to acquire money. Thus by making money by devious means, man only looks to amass comforts and luxuries. He loses himself in the search for luxuries every moment.

Ignorant people providing shelter to sins and immorality, leaving aside their real nature and good deeds, do not know that materialistic luxuries are ephemeral and induce indolence. Real happiness is inside man's conscience, which is always guiding him about right and wrong. The one who listens to his conscience always walks the path of virtue. Every person should know that there are no shortcuts to true success and that real success can only be achieved by systematic hard work with the right techniques. To brace your foundation, you need to reduce your desire for comfort and give priority to skill, capability and hard work.

4. Ignorance

In today's world, people are totally ignorant about their actual divine nature (Self), especially youngsters, who invite the fury of others due to their behaviour. This is all due to lack of character and ignorance. If man's greatest wealth were to be cited, it would be his 'character'. Youngsters today are seen flinging away their wealth of character carelessly. Fashion, bad company and aimlessness make them heedless towards their Foundation90.

Among all things sacred, sacredness of the conscience is most important. If you do not wipe out the vices growing inside you – like lust, anger, greed, attachment, jealousy and hatred – or do not rectify their direction through meditation techniques, then a big portion of your physical energy is wasted in them. These tendencies contaminate not only your body but also your feelings, mind, speech and actions. On one side this impedes your self-development, and on the other side the path to social and cultural progress gets blocked.

Today, mental deterioration has taken place in people due to ignorance. They have come to think that whatever their sins may add up to, all of them will be washed away if they visit some holy shrine. This mentality has been produced due to ignorance and the business interests of priests and clerics.

Till the time you do not realise that what you are holding in your hands are diamonds, you will carelessly be throwing them away thinking them to be ordinary stones. The educated youth of today oftentimes fall into bad company and waste their invaluable time, which later leaves them with nothing but repentance. In ignorance some fall prey to narcotics while some get addicted to liquor.

Sometimes youths develop such violent tendencies that they become a danger to the law and order of society. Doing wrong things in ignorance or getting habituated to substance abuse are signs of a weak foundation.

5. Falling for sensuous pleasures

Man is the master of five senses through his mind, but in absence of discipline, he keeps wandering to seek sensuous pleasures. The more oil you pour into the fire, more will the fire flare up. Man thinks that by gratifying the desires of his senses, he will feel satisfied. But eventually he found out that even after providing all pleasures to the senses, their cravings did not end; instead, after serving the senses, the bad tendencies of the mind increased even further. Thus, never go into the extremes of sensuous pleasures and tread the middle path. Maintain balance in the enjoyment of every sense.

Your sleep should neither be too much nor too less. Your meals should neither be too much nor too less. If you work and rest in proper measure and at proper intervals, you will not be a slave of your senses, but their master.

In pursuit of sensuous pleasures, man is turning his back on humanity, morality, naturalness and his own objectives. What should be done in this case? We need to awaken awareness within us towards the attraction of bodily pleasures. We need to exercise self-control and not indulge in the extremes of any pleasure. Very soon this will become our nature. In this way our senses will help to brace up our Foundation90 instead of undermining it.

6. Falling prey to laziness

All the powers of the human body become inactive only due to laziness. In spite of being energetic, man's body climbs aboard the boat of laziness, which remains tied at the bank of the river of life.

If you have the capacity to perform some task but if your body is lethargic, you can never complete your tasks. The task that has not even been started is obviously miles away from completion. Incomplete jobs give rise to excuses, excuses give rise to lies, repeated lies give rise to wrong tendencies and wrong tendencies give rise to lack of character. Thus you see how laziness makes man strike at his own foundation.

Laziness can become man's worst enemy because a lazy person does not even start doing his deeds. Without apt deeds, character does not develop. Therefore man should not show laziness in any task. The tasks may be household ones, job-related or social ones, he should not shy away from them.

To become a trustworthy person, one should get rid of not only bad behaviour but also his laziness. Only then can he perform the karma of improving the rest of his negative aspects. And only then can he think of developing a stronger Foundation90. Otherwise, people will look at his laziness and never believe that this person can execute the job on time.

7. Lack of moral values

Wrong moral values destroy man's Foundation90 even before it becomes strong. So first understand what are tendencies, patterns of thinking, and morality, and how they are formed.

There are two sheets of paper before you, one over the other. You have a pen in your hand. You write something on the upper paper and its imprints are seen on the lower paper. You see some lines imprinted on the lower paper. You can see them only by observing closely. This means that action was done on the upper paper and its subtle pattern formed on the lower paper. Everybody wrote something or the other on the paper, but everybody's patterns do not form alike. Some patterns are superficial while some are deep. If you run a paintbrush over the lower paper, you can see the fine white lines of those patterns.

The mind runs in these patterns. This is where it finds its food. This is where it sustains. Lack of good patterns or presence of bad patterns is an important reason for a weak Foundation90. Patterns are actually those activities that are done repeatedly, which then become the tendencies of a community or the whole society. Gradually those particular activities or habits are called as morality. Morality or moral values are transferred from generation to generation.

Faith towards good morality brings out the sense of responsibility even in difficult situations. Due to faith, good company and *sadhana* (spiritual practice), man develops a good morality. Consequently he becomes a good citizen and creates a better society. Lack of faith and tendency of suspicion tarnish the mind and hamper the creation of a good character. Good patterns (good habits) are required for strengthening Foundation90, which are also called culture or the wealth of morality. Moral values or morality is the means by which we decide the external and spiritual purity or impurity.

Moral values help in the setting up of a benchmark for recognising good or bad deeds. Human life becomes complete only on the strength of good moral values. The person who has no morality and no discriminative intelligence *(viveka)* does not feel any difference between the good and the bad. In the name of goodness, he will go on sinking in the mire of evil.

8. Materialistic media

Materialism and illusory attractions are advertised and advocated extensively in the world today. The advertisements propagating them have an impact on your thoughts. Advertisements in television, articles in newspapers, vulgar movies and books damage man's character because today these things have proliferated a lot in his life and influence him immensely.

This world is full of illusory sensuous attractions. A lot of things in this world are attracting man. At home, he reads advertisements in the newspaper and watches television.

These media constantly propagate and reiterate to him that the kind of life they are showing is the life he wants. Without even being asked, his friends too suggest him the same. The deep influence of advertisements has steadily left his personality, by which he is known, to be a mere object. Fancy cell phones, broadband, beautiful bungalow, exquisite lawn, luxurious car, glittering ornaments, expensive attire, etc. are the basis on which his character is judged. According to the beliefs of the society, the expensive stuff he has decide how powerful and glorious he is.

Personality is not that which tells us 'As long as I don't have a cell phone, I won't feel self-confident.' You can have selfconfidence even without these accessories. A few years back when there were no cell phones, people did have selfconfidence. Self-confidence is an inner quality, which does not depend on external objects.

A two-rupee newspaper predicts our day, our future, our life. We believe what is given in newspapers and think that we now know the truth. 'If it is printed in the newspaper, it has to be true' is our belief. Is it the truth? No. If you read your horoscope in some other newspaper, you will find something else printed there. Usually we read only one newspaper an we are not aware of what is written in other newspapers. Hence, don't believe everything printed in the newspaper to be the complete truth.

Movies too have a profound influence on our life. It is shown in films that one should have a girlfriend or a boyfriend, there should be many friends around, there should be a comic principal in college, a comic sergeant, etc. These movies show us an imaginary world and we begin to think that world to be true. This is the game and business of the illusory world of materialism.

Eight Consequences of a Weak Foundation90

An unsuccessful life is such

Foundation means the root or base, which provides support. If the foundation of a building is weak, it won't take much time to collapse. A small earthquake is enough to bring it down.

The strength of any house is assessed by its foundation. The foundation stones are not visible externally. Hidden inside, they go about their job of firmly holding the building in place. You can imagine the ill-effects if this foundation grows weak.

A lady once bought two saplings. She planted one in a pot and the other in the ground. Within a few weeks they started growing up. Whenever there was rain, strong winds or storm, the lady used to shield the potted plant to protect it from the elements. However, the other plant stood exposed and went through all the vagaries of nature. Enduring the storms, the roots of this plant became stronger. On the other hand, the potted plant became very delicate. It never gathered the strength to withstand storms.

One day the lady left the potted plant out in the open and went out to visit her relatives. Meanwhile a strong wind ensued followed by heavy downpour. The potted plant could not endure it and was uprooted. The other plant, rooted in the open ground, stood through it, because over the period, sustaining frequent storms, its roots or foundation had become extremely resilient.

Like the plant rooted in the open ground, we too have to make our Foundation90 (our character) absolutely solid so that any eventuality in life will not be able to bring down our level of consciousness, our intellect and our discriminative power (viveka).

Let us take a look at the effects of a feeble character. Sometimes the consequences of a weak Foundation90 can even be fatal.

1. Companies and banks going bankrupt

Many companies go bankrupt only due to the shaky Foundation90 of its personnel. A group of people start a private bank and collect money from the public. But there are some people in this group who do have a good Top10 (personality), but a flimsy Foundation90. These people make false assurances and tempt people by promising a high interest on their capital and attractive loans. Then their greed makes them fall short of their promises. Consequently the bank goes bankrupt and along with it all the investors. The staff that had been working for years together for the bank, come to face complete ruin. All this happens due to those founder members who have an unsound Foundation90.

2. Being duped by thugs

People with a weak Foundation90 very often indulge in wrong activities due to greed. Some shopkeepers price the same item differently to different people. If they sense that the customer is not going to bargain, they hike up the price. If they see smart or bargaining customer, they reduce the price a little. Other than such shopkeepers, some customers too swindle the shopkeepers. They tell the shopkeeper that they agree to whatever price they fix, and then dupe them with torn notes or counterfeit notes. The greedy shopkeeper caught unawares then realises that thugs have conned him and he did not even get a hint. Such shopkeepers do not know that they themselves attract those kind of customers. It is their greedy nature and inadequate Foundation90 that attracts similar people towards them.

3. Getting trapped in greed

Some people are very greedy for money. If anyone offers them a bribe, they immediately heed to such requests and get into illegal acts. Definitely, such people have an unstable Foundation90 and that is why they easily push through wrong activities. The truth of life is that whatever is ours, is definitely going to come to us, and nobody can stop it.

Suppose five hundred rupees are coming to you. Now these can come from under the table and can also come from over the table. Which way they come to you is dependent on your Foundation90. If your Foundation90 is wobbly, you easily accept money coming from under the table. If your Foundation90 is firm, you will say, 'If this money is mine, I do not want it from under the table. I want this money in the righteous way.' When you reject taking money from under the table, it is going to come to you through the other channel i.e. in the right way.

4. Falling for addictions

The repercussions of a frail Foundation90 fall on man's personal life too. Such a person easily falls into bad company and becomes a victim of substance abuse. He initially heeds to his friends' invitation for drink and smoke and then it becomes a habit for him.

He literally falls in the gutter under the influence of alcohol. He becomes so addicted to alcohol, that along with his own, he also makes the life of his family a living hell. He even puts his property and house at stake to carry on drinking and gambling. But he learns no lesson from this. Every other day he creates a hell for himself. In this way, a vulnerable Foundation90 can lead man to addictions and also ruin the life of his family members.

5. No control over the mind

A person with a vacillating Foundation90 has no control over his mind, which causes him to suffer several consequences in his life. Like, a person goes to a party and eats more than he can digest. He eats ten pieces of cake instead of two and falls ill the next day with indigestion. He becomes a slave of his taste buds and his other senses, and loses his health.

6. Money problems

People having a weak Foundation90 have no self-discipline. Consequently they always face shortage of money. Such untrained people have no knowledge of when, where and how to spend money. Even if they acquire a huge sum of money, they lose it in no time. These people don't understand that 'many little drops make an ocean'. Even a poor man, if self-disciplined, can surely save some money. A person saving money cannot remain poor for long. Being disciplined is itself a proof of a sound Foundation90. People having skill, talent, passion for work, courage and honesty do not face money problems for long.

Those having a limp Foundation90 never wish to start with small jobs. Hence they never get the opportunity to do bigger things. Such people get dejected and fall prey to bad tendencies. They wish to earn money without taking the efforts and therefore resort to unscrupulous methods. It is often seen that these people are low on self-confidence. They become pessimistic and keep crying about their ill fate. They consult astrologers and shy away from hard work. The desire to earn quick money by hook or crook leads them to lotteries and other such get-rich-quick schemes. They lose all their money and suffer at the hands of poverty.

7. Job problems

Due to inadequate Foundation90, people have to deal with problems at work. They are often inundated with thoughts like, 'The job I'm doing today is not permanent... I don't feel interested in this job... I can't do this job... I don't want to do this kind of a job... I feel bored doing this job... I don't even get perks in this job...'

Being victims of their mind, they change their jobs frequently. Such people cannot look at their life from a higher point of view. They never get the thoughts like, 'The job that I'm doing now is helping me in my inner progress, which will be useful in the highest expression of my self. So I must happily continue doing this job until I reach the next rung of the ladder of progress.' Do not change jobs just by looking at perks and opportunities to avoid hard work. Do not obey your mind and make your Foundation90 weak. You will then save yourself from numerous ill-effects.

8. Drifting away from God

A person with a feeble Foundation90 drifts away from God and forgets his true divine self. He forgets the purpose of being born on Earth, which is God-realisation or Selfrealisation followed by expression of the Self. His entire life is spent in attending a job, rearing children, raising them and building wrong kinds of relationships. Such people not only remain far away from God during their lifetime but also die without having known God.

On this Earth, several people bear the burden of their deeds and remain distant from God. They leave aside a happy natural life and burdening themselves with illusive responsibilities, they stressfully run their body, home and nation. ('Illusive responsibilities' because actually God is the doer of all actions and takes care of all our responsibilities.) Such people wail and whine all their life and exit the world without having known the whole-and-sole purpose of being born on Earth.

To know and achieve your purpose of life on Earth, consolidate your Foundation90. To do so, you can apply 13 remedies given in the subsequent chapters. In the next 13 days to come, utilise one remedy per day. These 13 days will be written in golden letters in your book of life.

Acquire the Quality of Enhancing the Primary Ten Qualities

Secret of knowing and appreciating qualities

FIRST REMEDY

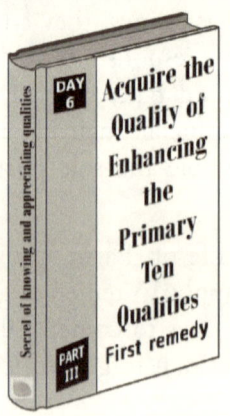

Every object in this world, whether small or big, living or nonliving, has its importance. On the basis of this understanding, start observing the good qualities in everyone and everything. By always looking at demerits in others, man remains feeble. People listening to and watching news channels and nattering about it all day long fall prey to this feebleness or vulnerability. People watching these news channels should be careful, lest they begin to see everyone with suspicion. Therefore, stop paying attention to negative things as far as possible. Watch and listen to positive news only. Learn to look out for and appreciate the beauty spread all around us.

A disciple always used to obey the instructions of his spiritual master. He always served his master with devotion and tried to imbibe as much knowledge as possible. One day he asked, 'Master, I am 25 today, isn't my learning over yet?' The master looked at him tenderly and said, 'Son, your learning is over, but the test of that learning is not over yet.'

'What test, Master?' asked the astonished disciple. The master replied, 'Go around in this jungle and find me such an herb that is not useful at all.' The disciple immediately set off on his search. In the evening he returned and said, 'Master, there is no such object in the jungle or in the whole world that is useless. Therefore, I did not come across any herb in the jungle that has no use.'

The Master was pleased and said, 'Son, your learning is complete now, because you have understood the importance of every particle of nature and the secret of knowing and appreciating qualities.'

This story illustrates the usefulness of every particle of nature. This also drives home the point that no person in this world is born without a purpose. Every human being has qualities. It is a different matter that due to the predominance of negativities in a given person, we feel that he has no qualities at all. Some qualities are definitely present in such a person too. Hence, each one of us should possess the art of recognising the qualities hidden in ourselves and in others.

Only a gemmologist has the eye for diamonds. If you too wish to become an expert gemmologist (successful person), try to recognise the diamond-like character inside you and do not treat it like a stone and spend it worthlessly along the roadsides.

Understanding the importance of character, everyone should now take an oath, especially the teachers who care about the future of children: 'While there is still time, we will impart the training of Foundation90 to our students. We will not just teach them theoretically, but will demonstrate it live by setting an example with our own good and strong character.'

Apart from parents, teachers also play an important part in shaping the character and future of youngsters. Therefore, in every school and college, youngsters must be taught that 'a successful person achieves success and remains successful only due to a sound Foundation90 or upright character.' Just the teaching of this one line can solve several problems of youngsters. If students do not learn this teaching during their educational years, they invite numerous problems into their life. This will not only have a bad effect on their life but also on their family, society and country at large.

For formation of character or integrity, every person must choose high qualities, which he can suitably adapt. He must constantly strive to incorporate these qualities fully into his life. Sooner or later he will definitely gain expertise and his character will begin to shine in the effulgence of these qualities. The ten primary qualities can be along the following lines:

1. Desiring welfare of all – impersonal, selfless feeling
2. Acquiring maximum knowledge on a particular subject – becoming an expert in a given field
3. Self-study – studying yourself and your thoughts through self-observation and self-introspection
4. Patience – ability to control tendencies, becoming an expert in the practice of patience
5. Punctuality – being foresighted and completing your work on time
6. Being steadfast on your principles – always keeping your goal before your eyes
7. Taking responsibilities – mustering courage to take on new responsibilities
8. Keeping promises – always fulfilling your commitments
9. Being honest and happy always – not selling your integrity
10. Maintaining purity of mind – keeping away from bad thoughts, feelings or intentions

Without a firm foundation, no one can attain success in life. An individual with a deficient foundation will crave for success, and time and again will moan about his ignorance of Foundation90 and Top10, and repent that 'if only someone had told me about it at the right time, I would have worked on it...' But it is not too late for you... if you have decided to completely read this book... and resolved to implement it.

Imbibe good qualities

To enhance your Foundation90, imbibe good qualities. If a smoker resolves to quit smoking, then on breaking this habit, he will achieve so much happiness, which he had never achieved even by smoking.

Ask yourself, 'What are the demerits within me that I need to remove? What are the qualities I need to imbibe? What are the qualities I have that I need to preserve?' These qualities can be faith, patience, good communication skills, human relations, work efficiency, etc. Imbibe all these qualities and become dependable and trustworthy.

Avoid covering up for others' character deficiencies

Those, who wish to brighten up their character and guard the wealth of integrity, should not help in others' wrongdoings. This is often seen in colleges.

A boy wants to bunk studies and go loafing around town. He asks his friends not to tell about it to his parents. Some of them help him in this and lie to his parents saying, 'Your son has gone to the library [or a friend's place] for studying.' It was then seen that the character of those people who helped him in his wrongdoings also became poor. They too started doing the same kind of things. As the saying goes: *An honest enemy is better than a dishonest friend.*

Do not support to cover up for others' character deficiencies and in turn damage your Foundation90. Always help those people, with whom you come to know of your shortcomings and the solution to overcome them. The next solution is the solution to overcome the weakness of not being able to hear about your weakness.

DAY 7

Self-introspect

Remove the weakness of not being able to listen about your weaknesses

SECOND REMEDY

The Top10 of every person, i.e. his external appearance, helps him initially but later on it's only his Foundation90 that works for him.

You have to learn the art of selfintrospection to make your Foundation90 gigantic and mighty. Self-introspect and look at the thoughts arising in your mind. It is our thoughts that give us an idea about whether our Foundation90 is strong or weak. Let us understand this with the help of an example.

There was a man who never stole anything in his life. One day, he stumbled upon a large amount of money. But he did not steal. What can be the reason? Did he really not get any thought of stealing it or was there some other reason? The reason he did not steal the cash was that at that time a thought appeared in his mind, 'Is anybody watching me? I might get caught.' That means the thought of stealing did arise in his mind, but he did not do so due to the fear of being caught.

Understand from this example that during any incident, the thoughts arising in your mind tell whether your Foundation90 is sound or unsound.

If a rich man comes to find a bundle of cash, he may say, 'Look, I am so honest; there's so much money lying before my eyes and I am not taking it.' It is a good thing that he did not steal the money; but it is not some extraordinary merit, because he is already a rich man, there's no dearth of money for him. If a poor man were to stumble upon the money and if he does not take it in spite of needing it badly, then it is definitely a big deal. It shows that his Foundation90 is unshakeable.

If someone finds a hundred rupee note, what will he do? He may go about searching for the owner and duly return it. What if he finds 1000 rupees? What if he finds 10,000 rupees? Will he be able to return the money? If he hesitates to return 10,000 rupees, it means that the strength of his character is worth only Rs. 10,000. Every person should ask himself, 'How much is the strength of my character worth? What is the worth of my integrity?'

From time to time, everybody should ask himself such questions and, through self-introspection, contemplation and self-observation, cleanse his conscience. Read the biographies of great men of the world and take inspiration from them. This will help remove all the faults present inside you. Remove the feelings of guilt due to mistakes committed by you and make your mind neutral and pure.

Make every mistake your teacher, i.e. learn from every mistake. Consider every instruction of your guru to be a prophecy. This will help in creating a high and ideal character. Each of us should dream of scaling this height.

Take your feedback from people

When people give a negative feedback about some job you have done, it is a good thing. Whenever you receive a feedback from people, learn to use it to your advantage. Do not ignore the feedback. If anything comes to you, it does so because it is your need. You need the feedback that people give you. Maybe you don't need it in the manner that people hand out to you, but you should ignore the manner and learn to take advantage of the feedback. Don't assume that if someone gave you an apple, you must eat it. Perhaps the papers on your desk are flying and the apple was meant to be used as a paperweight!

You may think, 'My health is fine; then why am I being given this health magazine?' But there could be some other reason why you were given the health magazine. Therefore, do not hesitate in taking it. After taking it, think of how it can be utilised.

There is not a single thing in the world that is useless. Hence, take every feedback and learn to utilise it in the appropriate way.

With the analogy of the book, you would have understood what kind of a book you are and how your Foundation90 is. If any chapter is wrong in your book, you can set it right by editing it. To do so, form a group (good company) and take apt feedback from everyone.

In a proper group, you should be able to tell, 'This is my book (my life). Look at it, read it and definitely give me a proper feedback.' If anybody wants to give you a proper opinion about your book (life) and you ignore him, you are committing a big mistake. To develop a powerful character, it is imperative to know your defects and bring them to light. There are some imperfections in man which he cannot realise by himself. Only the feedback from true friends can help him know about such subtle imperfections and eliminate them.

Whether or not people tell you about your blemishes, you should definitely take an honest opinion from everyone. If there is someone who is higher than you, ask him, 'How is my Foundation90, how is my Top10, and what are the things that I need to guard against?' When someone is able to tell you honestly about yourself, you can work on his feedback and become an exquisite book (person).

What is written inside your book and what is hidden? How can this be revealed? It can be revealed by your style of printing. How is your printing? When people look inside your book, what should they get to see? You have to decide this. That means your behaviour with people should be such that by looking at you, they should be inspired to strengthen their Foundation90 too. Therefore, never hesitate in asking for feedback from others.

The secret of strengthening Foundation90

Just as Foundation90 becomes firm by imbibing good qualities, similarly by bringing your flaws to light and improving on them, your Foundation90 can become strong too. Do not leave any stone unturned in finding out your flaws and improving on them. Become a professional in uncovering your flaws. Nobody can make his Foundation90 sturdy by hiding his faults from himself. Rising above shortcomings and imbibing good qualities – this is the secret of strengthening your Foundation90.

Those, who want to fortify their foundation, always wish to know about themselves and their mistakes from successful people. Usually no one likes to listen to his mistakes and flaws from others, but without knowing your mistakes, you cannot improve upon them. Some mistakes are such that you cannot see yourself, but your well-wishers can. When you wish to learn from your mistakes, you will ask others about their feedback on you. When you are being praised for your good qualities as well as being informed about your failings, first collect the information about your failings. Praise of good qualities will go on; but getting stuck with appreciation, do not put a curtain over your negative aspects.

DAY 8

Let Your Aim be the Pilot of Your Life

Make the right choice between aim and gain

THIRD REMEDY

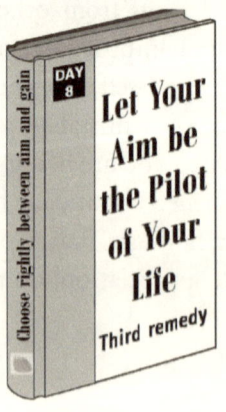

The aim of every human being is: To do what he can do. To become what he can become. To fulfil the purpose for which he is born on Earth.

If you are not born with the purpose of becoming a President, don't even try to become one. Even if you do become the President, you will be the world's unhappiest President. We can attain true happiness by becoming only what we want to become. You do not have to think of what others can become nor compare with others. A lily doesn't think, 'Why am I not like a jasmine or a rose?' So, become what you are. Become that which makes you ever happy. Become complete.

Relation between aim of human life and Foundation90

Every flower in the garden is blossoming. It is a different matter that before blossoming completely, some flowers break off, some are blown away by the winds, some are plucked out by someone and some get infected with worms or diseases. But the aim of every flower is to blossom completely and to spread its fragrance to one and all. Just like a flower, the aim of every human being is to completely blossom, open up and spread the fragrance of his qualities all around him.

If you wish your Foundation90 to become strong, let your aim be the pilot of your life. Make your pilot very powerful, i.e. set a powerful aim for yourself, because without aim the plane of life cannot head in the right direction.

Decide the name of your book

Give your book (life) a beautiful name that you want and work on it consistently. According to the name (aim) you have given to your book, you will have to put in that kind of work. After deciding the name of your book, your focus should be on the following aspects: 'Those who read my book should get these particular benefits, the people who are with me should progress in these particular ways, and for that I need to develop these particular qualities and eliminate these defects.' At the same time you should also have the understanding regarding 'actually whose expression is taking place… what are we believing ourselves to be (as the body?) in every incident and giving a response… how strong has our Foundation90 become…?'

When you keep working upon the aim of your book, effective results will show up. Sometimes in between the outcome of old seeds and patterns will pop up but now you have acquired the method of destroying them in the right way. Until you see a new scene and a new morning rise, you have to consistently work on the aim of your book without getting caught up in illusory truths.

With a strong Foundation90, you can break all your hardened tendencies and habits, even if they have been formed due to your upbringing or even if they were in your genes. If you have decided a powerful aim of your life, nothing is impossible for you. You have to develop your character in such a way that when people look at your book (you), they are reminded of such things as divine devotion, love, strength, courage, happiness, contentment, creativity…

More powerful your aim, more is the strength and support you will get from people. When you are prepared to live an impersonal life, when your aim is for the well-being of all, then everybody becomes ready to help you. When man works only for personal gains, very less people co-operate with him. Therefore, make an impersonal aim and let your book (life) benefit all.

The whole aim of human life is to blossom, open up and express oneself fully, i.e. to achieve your highest possibility. A person's complete aim is achieved when he completely blossoms, opens up and freely plays the game of life.

Very few people set up an aim of their life and even fewer write it down. A responsible person does not keep his aim only in his head, he writes it down with a systematic plan in his diary. You too must write down the aim of your life, by reading which you feel excited and happy, by reading which you feel inspired and courageous to work on it, and all your fears run away.

By deciding on an aim, the mind stops wandering, which results in Foundation90 becoming stronger. History shows that those people who succeeded on the strength of their character had a powerful aim. If you do not have an aim, you will not be able to keep your Foundation90 firm for long.

Set a powerful aim

When you get an aim, no difficulty in the world will seem like a difficulty to you. Else, an aimless person gets upset over every little matter such as not getting his glass of milk at bedtime or not getting his favourite pillow, without which he cannot get to sleep. Every little inconvenience upsets him.

Give yourself an aim. Don't sit waiting for life to give you an aim or expect that someone will come to you and tell you your aim. Don't depend on anyone; you yourself decide your aim. The day that you set your aim will be a golden day of your life because you gave your life a direction on this day by deciding your aim. Without direction, man's hapless state continues.

With the right direction and an inspired aim, a virtuous person's capabilities improve to such an extent that he is able to gain expertise very easily in those aspects which he was not able to do earlier. For instance, a person was not even able to type a single word, but after understanding the importance of qualities like responsibility, honesty, commitment and love, he is now able to take up a big role in the making of books. How did this transformation take place? By setting the highest aim of life, it is possible for anyone to do this. With the strength of character, you can do big things through your book (life).

Higher the aim we set, greater is the energy that nature provides us with. People who understand this principle of nature never aim small. If you want to feel the power of nature inside you, give yourself a high aim and begin to do the important tasks that can be done at present.

Set an aim and change your life

The priorities in your life will change after you get an aim. If you cannot spare much time for your health, if saving money is difficult for you, if you never think of others' needs, if teamwork and time management is difficult for you, then with setting up an aim it is possible that you devote your time to each one of these aspects. It is also possible that after getting an aim, your daily routine may change entirely. Hence, before anything else, give your life a powerful goal.

The aim of someone's life could be to become a doctor, engineer, carpenter, musician, acquiring capabilities, etc. If you wish to become a carpenter, go ahead and be a good, successful carpenter. If you have decided to become a doctor, become a good doctor and acquire as much knowledge of medicine as possible.

Consider character-building to be your responsibility and aim Developing a good character is your responsibility. However, this does not mean that you have to keep thinking 24 hours about your character. Developing a good character means first knowing that character and integrity is your wealth, and living life on its basis. While carrying on your daily activities, you have to conduct yourself in such a way that your Foundation90 becomes sturdy and unshakeable.

Building character is our responsibility. Everyone needs to understand this responsibility. Youth today are more concerned about beautifying their external appearance than thinking about character-building. This is why the knowledge of character and integrity in today's generation is getting extinct.

You see on channels like Discovery that some particular species are getting extinct. Some people then come forward and take measures to protect them. The government too helps in this cause. It builds sanctuaries and forests for them so that they are saved from extinction. If so much can be done for an animal, why not for the knowledge of character? Why not for saving Mission Earth from extinction?

Knowledge is limitless. It is like the pearl in the ocean which cannot be gained just by diving in, but by deciding the appropriate direction. Until and unless we recognise the power hidden inside us and decide the course of our conduct, our direction and our work system, we will not find success.

Gain and aim are different

The body that we have received has its importance, but if someone forgets the real purpose of life and spends his entire life in adorning his body, there cannot be a greater folly. The pages of history carry the names of only those people who have accomplished such work that revealed their virtuous character. Such people are known not by the beauty of their body but by their character and work. The body has its own gains but to consider the body to be everything is ignorance.

Gain and aim are two different things. If you gain from something, it doesn't mean that that itself is your aim. The gains brought by the body do not enhance the wealth of character, in fact they degrade it. You do benefit by going to a beauty parlour, you feel good and fresh, but it doesn't build your character. When we move our attention away from our character, it is then that we begin to consider the body to be everything.

People wish to use their physical beauty and reach the summit of success in life. Some people do accomplish this, but their purity of mind gets lost. With power in hand and lack of wisdom, man's mind does not remain pure; it gets corrupted. Such people do achieve success but lose the wealth of integrity. The one whose mind is not pure, his character also does not remain virtuous. As against this, some people do not reach the pinnacle of success in life, but they do have purity of mind. Such people have the treasure of character and that is why they set out on the path of Truth. You need courage to walk the path of Truth, and only those people have courage who have the wealth of character. Keeping the wealth of character intact is a big responsibility. Today the time has come to educate people right from school and college about this subject so that they can decide the right aim in life and earn the wealth of a moral life.

DAY 9

Bright Untruth and Dark Lies

Learn from every mistake

FOURTH REMEDY

On this new morning, awaken from the unconsciousness of dark deceit and lies. When man lies or deceives someone due to some reason, the act of lying or deceiving happens unconsciously. The utilisation of lies should not take place in the darkness of unconsciousness, but in light.

When lies are told in darkness, it Learn from every mistake impairs the Foundation90. There appear some circumstances in life where man is forced to speak untruth. In such situations, always take care to see if it is a 'bright untruth' or a 'dark lie'.

Bright untruth

There could be some circumstances in which man needs to speak the untruth due to love or due to wisdom. Like, if some person you know is lying on his deathbed and asks you some questions. And for his reassurance, you need to lie to him. In such a situation, the act of speaking the untruth is not inappropriate. The person has only a few days left; one lie from your side can help him spend his last few days in peace.

If you speak the truth instead, he might die before his time. Knowing his sentimental nature, when you speak the untruth, there is nothing wrong in it. Sometimes when a doctor speaks the untruth to his patient, there is understanding behind this act. The doctor does not harbour malice towards his patient or anything like it, but he may need to lie due to love and understanding towards his patients.

The second type of situation where untruth is justified is where the intention is right. Therefore it is important to know the intention due to which a person is lying. If someone lies for the sake of his personal gains, it will be harmful for him. But if he lies without any kind of selfishness, and for the good of the person he is lying to, then it is not wrong, because his intention is not wrong.

The third reason is *'tej'** or bright. The lie uttered for the sake of welfare of people at large, is not wrong.

Thus we understood the circumstances in which speaking lies is not morally wrong and may be called as 'bright untruth'. This kind of

---

*Tej is one of the most important words coined by Sirshree. 'Bright' is the closest translation of this word. Let us understand Bright or Tej with the help of an example. There is happiness and there is unhappiness. Here happiness means opposite of unhappiness. But there also exists happiness that is beyond both these polarities. That is called Tej Happiness or Bright Happiness. This means that when the word 'Tej' or 'Bright' is used as an adjective, then the word that it describes as 'Bright' is beyond both polarities or beyond duality.

lies is spoken with full consciousness for the good of others and thus the word 'bright untruth' points towards light.

Dark lies

The two main reasons why man blatantly speaks a lie are attachment and lethargy. Some people lie due to attachment with certain people. And some people lie due to their indolent nature. They want to avoid work and say that they have done the work assigned to them, when they have actually done nothing. This habit of lying makes man's foundation hollow and vulnerable with every passing day. So whenever you lie to someone, ask yourself first whether it is a 'bright untruth' or a 'dark lie'.

Every person needs the understanding of bright untruth and dark lies in order to bolster his Foundation90. Oftentimes people who lie think that they are doing it for the good of others. But you must honestly discuss with yourself whether you are really doing good or doing bad.

Man is an expert in making his lies logical. He lies first and then proves his lies to be right. If man contemplates before speaking any untruth, every decision of his proves to be correct.

A boy once did not attend school. To protect him, his friend told his parents, 'Your son was definitely with me in the classroom.' What kind of a lie is this? This other boy thinks that he is helping his friend and backing his friendship. But in reality he is harming his friend because there is no understanding in his act.

Man should know in advance the understanding with which he is lying. Before lying, if he knows that it is a bright untruth and not a dark lie, he can go ahead with it. Otherwise, the tendency to lie gradually enfeebles his Foundation90.

Every person has to make his Foundation90 mighty. If Foundation90 is tough, whatever is printed inside will come out. That which is hidden (the Zero Experience), will grow, expand, and spread.

Every deed done by man brings him a fruit of either joy or sorrow. The benefit of lies is seen immediately, that is why lies keep on increasing. But gains that are instantaneous in nature prove to be harmful later on. Hence do not indulge in such momentary gains. People who lie to hide their mistakes do not stop lying because they do not see the results of speaking the truth at once. So they continue speaking one lie after another. They retort, 'Look, I started speaking the truth but I haven't yet seen any benefit from it.' They are told, 'Continue with the truth. Do not hide your mistakes, learn from them. Let every mistake help you progress. Stop repeating the same mistakes again and again.'

An entrepreneur wanted a salesman for his business. He shortlisted two candidates after a round of interviews. He seated the two of them next to each other and asked them questions. He asked, 'We want to sell our product in a given city. How should we begin?'

The first candidate was inquired, 'Have you been to that city?' He replied, 'Yes, I have been there. It's a terrible city, full of thieves and pickpockets. I had gone there three times and on all three occasions, my wallet was stolen.' The entrepreneur said, 'Is it?! When you went there, where did you stay?' The candidate answered, 'I stayed at a lodge. The food there was awful too. Please do not launch your product there.'

The second candidate was asked the same question, 'Have you been to that city?' He replied, 'Yes, I have been there too. Whatever he is saying is absolutely true. There are really many pickpockets around in that city. Even my wallet was stolen the first time. The second time I had to be very careful and only then I was able to save my wallet. The food at the lodge was terrible too. There is a lot of filth around. I was very upset with all these things the first time I went there. But the next time onwards, I always took tinned food along.'

The entrepreneur hired the second candidate because he saw that he learns from his mistakes. The first candidate's wallet was stolen three consecutive times; this was the height of foolishness. Despite knowing that it was coming, he did not keep a watch on his wallet.

The person having a feeble Foundation90 always goes through such things because he is not thoughtful. He does not focus where he should. It is natural for man to make mistakes, but if one is repeating the same mistake again and again, it means that he is not learning anything at all from his mistakes.

Which candidate would you have chosen? You would definitely have chosen the one who is learning from his mistakes. Every person needs to have this quality in order to become virtuous.

A person falls ill time and again, but keeps repeating the same mistake in his eating habits. It is possible that you commit these kinds of mistakes. Do not fear mistakes, but do not hide your mistakes behind the curtain of lies. Ask yourself, 'What should be done now in this situation? If I am committing this mistake, then how can I improve on it?'

Understand your lies and mistakes, learn from them and come out of them. It is fine if you commit a new mistake, you can learn new things from those mistakes and then free yourself from those mistakes. Freeing oneself from old mistakes and lies is essential for every such person who wants to make his Foundation90 absolutely formidable.

Beware of Unhealthy Entertainment

Employ 10 steps for healthy entertainment

FIFTH REMEDY

A major cause of a weak Foundation90 is unhealthy entertainment. Every person is in search of love and happiness, and to achieve this, without thinking he runs towards the world of entertainment.

In this era of advanced science, new discoveries are the order of the day. These new appliances and gadgets have changed the lifestyle completely, right from eating habits to Employ 10 steps for healthy entertainment identity of individuals. Science has lined up a full range of comforts before man. The discoveries that provide people with healthy entertainment and comfort are beneficial to mankind. But due to the conscienceless nature of man, these inventions are being utilised in a negative way. Devices like the television, computer, internet and cell phones have opened a new dimension of communication, but the uncontrolled or unbounded conduct of man has turned this blessing into a curse. Today, obscenity in television programmes and advertisements is escalating by the day. The condition is such that people feel hesitant to watch television together with their family. They know that what is being served does not fit into good moral values nor in our traditional values.

Revealing clothes and double-meaning jokes not only cause a decline in people's morality, but also force them to waste their valuable time. Hence, do not aimlessly watch all the programmes on television; watch only a few selected ones that will help in your goal. Do not forget your progress in the face of entertainment.

The current generation of youngsters is getting lazier by the day. They even wish for entertainment to reach their homes. The craze of watching television has engulfed the young generation. The daily soaps being shown on television are seen by the grandmother in the house as well as the daughterin-law. It is okay to an extent if the old grandmother watches them, because her life has almost passed her by. But sitting on her lap, her granddaughter too watches all the programmes. If the granddaughter is being raised in this manner, what kind of life will she create on growing up?

It is shown on television that a family is very gloomy. Suddenly they hear music being played. All the family members look out of the window and they see in the opposite house that people are drinking Coca-Cola and dancing and having fun. So their mantra for happiness is – 'Coca-Cola'. Looking at this scene, people are deluded into thinking that those who drink Coca-Cola are a happy exciting family, and those who don't are a dull family and have a dull life.

Then a film star appears on television and declares: 'You must have **this** car, this is a complete family car.' People begin to feel that it is necessary to have all these things in the society we live in, else this life is worthless.

All the programmes and advertisements on television and in newspapers tell us: 'Use this shampoo and enhance your image... Wear these clothes and people will be impressed by your image... Use this toothpaste and your teeth will shine like pearls and people will love to be in your company...' Advertisements of appliances and cars make us believe that by using these items, we can live a grand life. In this way, our mind undergoes new but wrong programming. Television, movies and newspapers are responsible for our programming, which already have us in their grip. We have been hypnotised by them, as it were. It is only a myth that we need a lot many things to live. Actually, a simple life is possible even with very few possessions.

Apart from television, video and internet, another thing that has people in its grip is the cell phone. A major portion of people's time is spent in sending and receiving messages. They do not realise what complications they are creating for themselves. Disaster lingers over their foundation due to this behaviour. Some people keep changing their mobile phones just to show off their false pride. They feel excited looking at and showing new mobile phones. When they get some time off from their mobiles, they jump right into the mesh of the internet and keep surfing for hours together.

To boost unhealthy entertainment and to show off, some people take heavy loans despite inability to afford them, and freely spend money in lavish weddings and parties. They do not hesitate even a bit in taking loans to show off false pride. And then to repay the loans, they have to resort to illicit ways. Day by day, man debilitates his foundation in this way.

Such people go bankrupt in this cycle of showy pleasures. They are not able to understand that if they didn't have the money, they were not supposed to indulge in all those things. If they were able to understand this, their life would have been easy, simple, straightforward and moral. They would have been able to take easy decisions.

The fact is that man does not want to feel bored even a single moment, hence he wants thrill and excitement in every activity, by which he can attain happiness (false happiness). But this ignorant fellow does not know that he is actually distancing himself from the love and happiness that he is searching for. The joy and the love which man is anxiously seeking is right inside him.

Ten steps for healthy entertainment

Instead of indulging in any unhealthy entertainment, man should search for some healthy entertainment for consolidating his foundation, such as:

1. Through the practise of yoga and pranayam (breathing exercises), experience the beautiful feeling of a healthy body. Experience the feeling of walking on clouds all day long.

2. Practise Silence Meditation *(moun sadhana)* and dive into real happiness.

3. Learn music and let go of all your tensions and apprehensions. Taking inspiration from music, include rhythm and harmony in your life.

4. Read good books and provide your intellect a proper diet. Through books, you can meet the world's greatest men sitting at home. A small book will bring them into your living room. You can know about the thoughts of these people and bring enthusiasm into your life. Then you will not feel the need for any unhealthy entertainment.

5. Join a hobby class. Explore new dimensions of life. Utilise your favourite game or hobby in a creative way. Ask people about their hobbies. They will be pleased to meet you.

6. Go to a laughter club. Laughing out heartily helps your health and it is good utilisation of time. You feel a new energy by laughing together with others. Don't laugh at people, make people laugh, and laugh *with* them.

7. Learn a new skill by joining a class. Always keep on learning for self-development, you will never feel old.

8. Go for a walk in the beautiful ambience of early morning. Look at every scene as if you are watching it for the first time.

9. Try to portray your feelings on canvas. Along with learning painting, you will also achieve good mental health.

10. Try to express your feelings through words, stories, poems or hymns. This will not only help you but also those who read them.

The ten steps given above will not only help in your development but also provide you with healthy entertainment.

If you wish your foundation to become powerful enough to enable you to take on any problem with ease and selfconfidence, liberate yourself from unhealthy entertainment and excitement today itself. Or at least start reducing it. Gradually, with patience, you will definitely achieve Destination Strong Foundation90.

DAY 11

Choose the Right Friends

Don't sit under a toddy palm tree

SIXTH REMEDY

Have a look at the shelf in which your book of life is placed, because the books in your vicinity tell a lot about you.

When you go into a big bookstore, you see various sections according to different subjects. For example, literary books, cheap books, story books, novels, books on psychology, philosophy, self-development, spirituality, etc. It is also important Don't sit under a toddy palm tree among which books is your book kept. By looking at the books around you, the customer understands what kind of a book you are. If the books around you are good, your importance goes up and the trust people have in you increases. People come to know that this person stays with good people and therefore he must be good, and if he stays with ruffians he must be bad.

A person, who goes to the bar frequently just to accompany his friend and not drink himself, cannot keep himself from drinking for too long. Thus, just as good company strengthens your Foundation90, the same way bad company weakens it.

Your choice of friends reveals your character. A philosopher named Emerson has said: 'Tell me the names of your friends, and I will tell your character. Your character can be inferred by the character of your friends.' It is said so because you tend to make friends with those similar to you. If you like to stay in ignorance, you will befriend those who speak in ignorance.

'Birds of a feather flock together.' Such proverbs make people stop and ponder. Now stop for a minute and think of what your friends convey about you. If someone went up to meet your friends, what kind of an opinion will he form about you? If you feel that he will form a negative opinion, it means that it's time to change your friends.

If an unwise and egoistic person were to choose his friends, he will choose those who are less knowledgeable than him, because in their company the egoistic person feels good, he feels superior. We feel superior among people who are less knowledgeable than us and inferior among people who are more knowledgeable and wiser than

You may have also seen in school that intelligent kids sit with other intelligent ones and weak kids sit with other weak ones, because that is where they feel good, or rather that is where they feel comfortable. If weak kids sit alongside intelligent ones, they feel stressed out looking at all the activities of the intelligent students. Their system, their schoolbag, their handwriting, their pens and pencils, their orderly and disciplined approach in everything makes them feel that they should either change their place or change themselves.

To empower your character, it is better to change yourself rather than change your place. Only by doing so, man can start working on his character. Looking at the systematic work and the qualities of the intelligent kids, the weak ones start feeling that they must overcome their weak points and develop their qualities.

True meaning of friendship

True friends are those that together walk the path of Truth. Radiance is added to your character by treading the path of Truth.

A true friend is the one who restrains his friend from doing wrong deeds, shows him his demerits and inspires him to tread the path of Truth. Only in the company of such friends can you rightly build your character. Else, among false friends you will lose your priceless treasure of character.

Even if one among your friends has new and limitless thinking, you do gain by his thoughts. If, in the group, this person talks about integrity or some new creation, the others immediately begin to think on those lines.

Let us now learn about the five types of friends and which is the group we are in.

1. **Phoney friends (Bentex friends):** Phoney friends means those friends that are fake. They appear to be as pure as gold externally (just like Bentex jewellery) but they only cause you harm. You must have seen many such specimens around, who were considered as friends but ultimately became the cause of downfall.

2. **Expensive friends:** Expensive friends are those who always need to be showered with treats. You only have to talk about going to some restaurant or a picnic or a party with them. Without this, they never come with you. They are ready to accompany you only as long as you give them whatever they want.

If you have friends who always tell you that you are right in spite of you being wrong, what will happen? Such expensive friends will lead you to disaster. You will never get to realise your mistakes and thereby you will never feel the need to work on improving your foundation. Expensive friends always say 'you are right', because they get food and drinks for free. If you are in the company of such friends, better beware.

3. **Cheap friends:** Cheap friends help you in inflating your ego and doing wrong things. Such friends just happen; they don't need to be made. They aid you in promoting dishonest activities. You mingle with such friends, engage in devious things and ask them not to tell anybody about your activities. Some of your friends may tell you, 'Don't tell anyone that I did this… don't tell this to my parents, don't tell that I bunk my studies… don't tell anyone that we were partying… don't tell anyone about my relationships…' You think you are being a good friend by complying with such requests and being an accessory in such activities. You are not! You are in fact helping in the degradation of your friend's character. You are not aware what will happen by hiding these wrongdoings. By getting caught up in the web of illusory pleasures, he will be ruined. At the moment he thinks that whatever he is doing is right. This is exactly like applying saccharin on the thumb of the child who has a habit of thumb-sucking. Such friends are cheap friends, guard against them.

4. **True friends:** True friends are those that make you complete, free you and make you an integrated person. In the company of such friends, your feelings, thoughts, words and actions all begin to fall in the same direction. These are true friends, good friends, who make you whole. A true friend is the one who does not aid in your wrongdoings, but brings you back on the right track. Only a true friend can help in the building of your character. Therefore, always stay in the company of true friends.

5. **'Bright' friends:** Bright friends are the ones who work like a mirror for you. They make you realise how every incident is an opportunity for you. They make you understand who you actually are; you realise your true divine nature by their guidance. You get a glimpse of your true self when you go in front of a bright friend. Where you realise your true self and the opportunity that you have got to attain the Supreme Truth and eternal bliss, there is your bright friend.

On meeting a bright friend, all the ignorance, illusions, delusions, infatuations and false beliefs in your life, vanish. Now you begin to see yourself clearly. A mirror only shows you your body, but a bright friend shows you what you actually are.

Whom to befriend and whom not to

To achieve your goal, take help from only those people who have the same goal as you. While climbing up a mountain join hands with those climbing up and not with those climbing down, because the one going up will also pull you along towards the top. The one going down will pull you downwards. If you want to become a doctor, staying in the company of doctors will help you in achieving your goal. Staying with engineers or teachers will not help your goal. Similarly, if you want to build your character and work on your Foundation90, stay in the company of those who have a strong Foundation90 and have already worked on their character.

Befriend those who are at least two steps ahead of you or equal to you in qualities (and not in wealth). By maintaining friendship with such persons, your possibility of building a virtuous character opens up, because they too know the importance of becoming virtuous. Thus both of you can build a virtuous character and lead a happy life. If your friend is already a virtuous person, it is very good for you because by staying in his company, you too can speedily build your character.

By staying in bad company, you too start imbibing their bad qualities. Man loses control over himself in bad company and indulges in things that degrade his character day by day. Thus the saying goes: 'Don't drink milk sitting under a toddy palm tree.' A toddy palm tree produces toddy, which is a type of liquor. Sitting under such a tree, even if you just drink milk, people will think that you are drinking toddy. More importantly, where will your attention be? Definitely, on the toddy tree. You start thinking about what you see. You start speaking what you think. Sooner or later you start doing what you speak. And bad karma (deeds) reap failure and misery. Therefore, do not sit under a toddy palm tree, enhance your maturity. The next solution unfolds the secret of enhancing your maturity.

DAY 12

Enhance Your Maturity

Become a complete person

SEVENTH REMEDY

When maturity comes into our life, our behaviour matures too. On maturing, we come to know how to behave with people in a given situation and a given place.

We behave in a particular manner from morning to night, from childhood to old age, at home, in the neighbourhood, in the society, in the state or country which is an indicator of our maturity. If our behaviour is not mature, it means that only our body has grown up; our mind and intellect have not.

Become a complete person

Children are hungry for love and therefore always want to attract everyone's attention towards themselves. They always wish to remain the centre of attraction. If children don't receive attention, they cry, brawl or do anything to attract attention. You know that children are small and immature, and that is the reason they behave so. Hence, you do not get distressed with their behaviour. But it is often seen that people behave like children even after growing up. They are only slightly more civilised than children. They do not realise that they are still childish in their disposition and that they are still behaving like a child who tries every possible means to attract attention.

In reality, only those people can be called as grownups who have understood the importance of character-building. They have understood that now they do not need respect wherever they go. If children show us respect, it is a good thing because they need to cultivate the habit of respecting elders. Do not help children in developing this habit in order to gain respect from them; help in it so that children acquire good qualities.

If you feel sad when you are not shown respect, it means that you are still immature; you haven't grown up. If you are ready to help others in spite of not being shown respect, it means that you have matured.

Children who don't receive attention during childhood, try something or the other on growing up to attract attention of others. For example, they devour on chocolates and ice-cream or keep eating something. Their basic desire is: 'I want something – something inside me. If not attention, then at least food.' Thus they constantly binge on goodies and put on weight.

There can be several other reasons why children put on weight, but a major reason is that man immaturely keeps on eating for want of attention. He feels satiated for a while, but you know how much time that food will remain in the stomach. It gets digested and he again craves for more… and more… Thus the child grows up physically, but does not gain maturity. He does not become an adult in the true sense.

Ask yourself the question, 'How much have I matured?' Some people might immediately proclaim that they are mature, but do not be hasty in your decision. Read everything given in this book and then decide how much percent you have matured. Then work on the shortcomings that you see in yourself to make your foundation solid.

Don't make a costly deal

An immature person always makes a costly deal. When you go shopping taking your kids along and your kid is hell-bent upon getting some toy he has liked, the shopkeeper doubles its price. He knows that you are definitely going to buy it because of your kid's obstinacy. In the same way an immature person always returns home making a costly deal.

Use your intellect to understand intellect

The accounting that man does with his intellect changes later on. The plans he used to make earlier are scrapped later. Whatever man thinks before liberation (moksh), changes totally after liberation.

A lady called up her husband from her parental home and said, 'Since the last one month you have forsaken me at this place. I have lost half my weight; when are you coming to take me back?'

Her husband made a calculation in his mind and answered, 'After one month.'

He is using his intellect to think what will happen after one month, but what is he focussing on? What kind of freedom does man want? Does he want freedom from some particular people and only then he will be happy? If that is the case, he is not yet intellectually mature.

Understand with the following examples how people converse if their intellect is not mature.

Example 1 : You have worn a wristwatch but it has stopped. Hence you ask a passer-by for the time. He replies, 'Why are you asking me when you have a watch?' You can understand that this person does not have intellectual maturity. He should understand that if you are asking for time in spite of having a watch, there must be some reason to it. There could be several other reasons why you were asking for the time. He should have just answered by telling the time, but instead he just revealed his immaturity.

Example 2 : You ask someone, 'Is this the Bajaj School?' He retorts, 'Can't you read? Look at the board!' You could have several reasons for asking. It's not that you can't read. If you have asked the question, he should reply. He shouldn't say, 'Don't you have eyes?'

Man behaves immaturely if his intellect has not developed. His answers reveal that he is yet a child. It's fine if you are just joking around with your friends, but if a stranger is asking you something, give him a proper answer.

Improve maturity at the intellectual level

On becoming mature, i.e. on attaining your highest possible state of development, your work will not feel like work. Whatever you do, at home or at your job, for the neighbourhood or for the society, it will not seem like a burden to you. Your work will feel like your self-expression and you will feel free due to that responsibility!

After achieving freedom, you have to choose: 'What should I do during the remainder of my life? How should I lead my life?' The one who has achieved freedom, delegates easy tasks to his subordinates and takes on the difficult job himself. He chooses the most difficult work for himself because now he has achieved total freedom physically and mentally. More the responsibility that man takes up, more is the freedom he experiences. And more the freedom he experiences, more difficult is the job that he takes up.

If a person takes up responsibility due to some greed or fear, then that responsibility feels like a burden to him. He cannot experience the joy of freedom with it. If you want to take responsibility, take it lovingly after attaining liberation so that it makes you feel happy and not burdened.

How does a mother take care of her child? Externally it appears to be a huge responsibility. The child troubles his mother endlessly, but the mother does not take this responsibility to be a burden, instead she takes it out of love. This is the way we have to fulfil our responsibilities, with love, and by becoming free.

Enhance your maturity with aware responsibility

'Understanding' and 'awareness' augments every man's foundation. If you have an irresponsible attitude towards any one aspect of your life, it affects every other aspect of your life too. Hence, take up the responsibility of developing every area of your life and make your Foundation90 proficient. Always ask yourself the question: 'How responsible am I and how irresponsible am I? How are my relations with my own family members, friends and relatives? Do I complete my work with full awareness or do I complete it in unawareness?'

After becoming a virtuous person, whatever responsibility you take, you will complete it with awareness. Mental and intellectual maturity is attained by 'understanding' and 'awareness', which helps in building an honourable character. The next solution will tell you about the secret of enhancing your mental maturity

DAY 13

Enhance Your Mental Maturity

Make your mind loving, pure and unshakeable

EIGHTH REMEDY

How to achieve mental maturity? Mental maturity means growing up mentally. When one achieves mental maturity, his mind becomes unshakeable. Then his mind does not waver under any circumstances. If the mind is not unshakeable, it flutters even by the sound of the doorbell. And immediately, negative thoughts begin in it – 'Another headache! Now who is this unwanted guest…?' A shaky mind gets ruffled at once in any situation.

If you had paused for a while before muttering negative words in your mind, you would not have been more upset than necessary. Since people do not have mental maturity, they get unduly worried, much more than required.

Make your mind loving, pure and unshakeable

To gauge your mental maturity, observe whether your mind has become loving and pure. A pure mind means that which is cleansed of all vices and impure feelings. When you look at people with a pure mind, you are filled with compassion and kindness. If you are able to keep your foundation strong in spite of achieving wealth, fame, status and power, it is a great thing. Else, people change when they achieve power. They speak differently. They speak with a hint of arrogance and irritation.

The one whose Foundation90 is strong, is free from evils like anger, jealousy, malice, arrogance, greed and hatred. His mind is pure. More impersonal your life, more is the purity of your mind. We have to ask ourselves whether the work we do is personal or impersonal in nature. Even the act of eating your food can be impersonal in nature. You eat so that your body can function. When your body supports you, you can happily work for the welfare of people.

Just as we remove dirt and stains from our clothes and make them clean, likewise we have to remove the blemishes from our mind and make it clean and sacred. We have to observe what all is happening with our mind. Is our mind on the way to become unwavering? If we are getting upset more than necessary during any incident, that itself indicates that we have not yet achieved mental maturity.

Fix a price tag to every incident

When you go to a shop to buy a matchbox and the owner tells its price as ten rupees, do you spare ten rupees to buy the matchbox? You don't, because you know that the shopkeeper is asking for more money than its actual value. In the same way, what can be the price of an incident occurring in your life? If some incident is quite upsetting, you should definitely get upset; but if you are getting upset too much even during a minor incident, it means that you are paying too high a price for that incident.

Suppose you once ask your neighbour for some tomatoes and she refuses. If you remain upset the whole day due to this minor reason, it will be understood that you do not have mental maturity. Such things are often seen to happen among housewives. These minor incidents disturb them a lot. They keep thinking – 'Yesterday she had taken some sugar from me… before that I had gifted her a dress… and now when I need something, she is flatly refusing… now let her come to me, I will teach her a lesson…' These types of thoughts leave them mentally distressed.

You do not know that the other person is not mature, and by expecting things from him you are hurting yourself. His aim and life are different. If you have come to know your highest aim of life and also have received the highest spiritual knowledge, then you have to be mature always. The opposite person may or may not be mature, but you have to enhance your mental maturity.

To mature mentally, we have to fix the appropriate price to every incident. Give only that much value to an incident that it is worth, not a penny more. Your neighbour did not give you tomatoes; you have to decide the price tag of this incident too. You have to ask yourself, 'How much is this incident worth?' If the answer you get is, 'This incident is worth ten minutes,' then remain upset for ten minutes, not more than that. When you look at the watch, you will realise that the distress is over much before ten minutes. This itself means that even ten minutes was a high price to pay for that particular incident. Applying this technique regularly, you will one day find that just by looking at the watch after a negative event has occurred, your distress vanishes. People return from a shopping spree and say, 'We got the goods at an economic price today.' But later they come to know that they could have got the goods for a much lower price.

Since man does not know the value of incidents, he continues to pay more for every incident. He never stops and thinks that he could be making a costly deal. A mentally mature person asks himself in every incident, 'This incident has taken place. Now, how much is this incident worth? Need I worry over this incident and let my temperature rise? Need my blood pressure rise? I will be upset only to the extent that I need to.' No incident is worth worrying about so much that your temperature or blood pressure shoots up. A little sweat trickling down and a little while of cheerlessness is enough. You don't have to pay more than this. When people don't have mental maturity, they speak of not forgetting incidents for eternity!

Only a happy person knows the right price of every event. Shopping should be done only by those who are happy. Else people go shopping to make the mind happy. Like, if their mood is down, they go shopping. In such a condition, they pay a higher price for the things they buy than their actual worth. They get a raw deal. People who go shopping because they are depressed or low on mood, later reveal that whatever they bought has never been used by them; everything is just lying around in their cupboards.

After achieving mental maturity, you will be able to take the right decision in the face of any storm of difficulty, because your mental strength will keep watering the cement of your foundation. Once the foundation becomes sturdy, every storm will be a mere puff of air that will keep coming and going.

Become Trustworthy

Reinforce your four strengths

<u>Ninth Remedy</u>

Become trustworthy, consolidate your foundation. To consolidate your foundation, become dependable in the eyes of people as well as your own.

Deliver what you promise. Commitment to our work demonstrates the might of our Foundation90. Commitment is a feeling in which along with courage, the heart and the brain are also utilised.

Courage is needed because it gives Reinforce your four strengths the motivation to work. When you say to someone, 'I am committed to do this work for you,' it means that you are definitely going to do that work. By making a commitment, your attitude towards your work becomes positive, because the main reason why man does not do some work is the negative attitude towards that work.

To commit is to stay firm on your promises regarding a given job. You may have heard the saying: 'A promise is a promise, no matter what.' It means, to take your work to its completion, you must cross every boundary, which will earn you respect as a dependable person. Follow the five indications given below to become dependable and trustworthy.

1. Catch time on time

Man becomes untrustworthy by telling one lie after another. To become trustworthy and dependable, one must fulfil his promises. Foundation90 becomes strong when you do what you say. Dependability empowers Foundation90. You will become dependable when you complete what you promise and catch time on time.

Be committed to complete your work within the decided period of time. Decide a date for the completion of every task you undertake, which is called as the 'white line'. White line is the time at which the work will be completed and come into light. If the work is not completed within the white line, you should contemplate over the reasons. What was it that you hadn't thought of? By contemplating this way every time, a time will come when you will see all your tasks getting accomplished within the white line.

When you do what you say, and you think what you do, and you speak what you think, all the powers of nature come together to help you and you become integrated and trustworthy.

Looking at the life of a disintegrated person, people do not feel certain whether he will be able to accomplish the task he has been given or not. While driving a car if such a person holds out his hand out of the window and gestures something, even this gesture is doubtful. Looking at it, you cannot make out whether he wants to turn right, turn left or stop and park his car. You cannot even guess what is in his mind. If you ask him, he will say that he did exactly what he was gesturing. He will give such wonderful excuses when asked about something, by which you will understand how frail his Foundation90 is. We have to ensure that we do not follow in his footsteps.

An undependable person always gives the excuse that he has no time. He does not realise that by giving such excuses of lack of time, he is losing his trustworthiness in the eyes of people. By losing his trustworthiness, he does not hesitate to keep evading things. Thus the circle of postponement and lack of trust goes on expanding.

If you want to be dependable, never give the excuse that you don't have time, because you have the same amount of time every day that any successful person has. If you don't aspire to achieve big successes, the least you can do is complete all your tasks on time.

Understand the value of time. Lost time can never be regained. Wasting time is wasting life. Higher your aim, higher is the need for you to learn the art of time management. Only after time management will your time be truly well-utilised.

The meaning of good utilisation of time is, 'completing the specified work on time'. Those who postpone today's work to tomorrow and tomorrow's work to the day after, are never able to fulfil their commitments. In this way they become untrustworthy and debilitate their Foundation90.

People waking up on time in the morning not only save themselves from the hassles and irritations of rush hour, but also reach their offices well on time and avoid the unnecessary troubles, running, screaming and stress. People who complete their jobs as per their commitments do not feel the load of the next job beforehand. They are ever ready to take on every job that they need to.

Do not overlook the need of the hour and do not procrastinate or try to escape from work. If anybody needs to be notified about something over the phone, do it immediately. You may feel awkward or insecure or your mind may not like it, but try it and see for yourself. Else if you keep avoiding minor situations like these, they later snowball into a big problem.

Man falters when he sees a new job coming before the end of the first job. However, with the intention of starting and ending the job on time, he always remains ahead of time and liberated from time.

Study the techniques of time management. When you go to bed at night, visualise in your mind the next day's tasks taking place. Think about the solutions to the likely problems in those tasks. When you do this, the next day you will actually see all your tasks getting completed on time and you will thus honour your commitments. Else, in due course you will lose the trust people have in you.

2. Be the author of your diary

A successful person has the quality of writing down his goal, his work and his thoughts. This quality also contributes to the solidity of your foundation. The one, who does not know the importance of becoming trustworthy and dependable, does not maintain a diary of his tasks and forgets many of his tasks. The technique of writing down tasks is very effective. It is extremely useful in breaking the habit of procrastination or forgetfulness.

People, who have resolved to become trustworthy, always write down their tasks. They have the insight as to why they need to complete their decided tasks on time.

Write down the work you have in hand in your diary, calendar, computer or cell phone. Make a list of your tasks and resolutions. Assign the right priority and white line to every task or resolution and make sure you complete it.

Accomplishing any task on time proves your dependability. With inspiration from every success you attain, you do not forget to do even the smallest of tasks. This habit makes you dependable in the eyes of people due to which they extend their whole-hearted co-operation to you.

Develop the habit of writing down everything. Many people do write diaries, but there is a proper method to it. If you write in the proper way, you stand to benefit a lot from it in the future. Learn the method of using a diary from those who have successfully utilised the efficacy of diaries.

A person told his friend, 'I now write down all my tasks in my diary. I no longer need to think about when to do which task.' The friend was impressed and replied, 'That's great! But what are you looking here and there for?' The person said,

'I'm searching for my diary.' From this anecdote, it is illustrated that if you are using a diary, you should know where it should be placed and when to open and read it. If you have written all your tasks in your diary and you cannot find your diary, then all the benefits you should be getting from it shall not be received. If you wish to become dependable, the habit of writing a diary will go a long way in helping you.

Always focus on how to handle the responsibility you have been handed in the best way. Without fearing the present responsibilities, take full advantage of them. Work can be accomplished remorsefully too, but that is not the way we want it. Break the old habit of carrying out work ruefully and develop a new habit of doing work with happiness and smiles. Write down the thoughts, merits and demerits that you find in yourself while working, so that later they can be utilised for overcoming your shortcomings.

3. Decide to take a decision, learn the art of taking decisions

If you want to become dependable and earn major success, you must learn well in advance the art of taking decisions. Else the situation later will be like digging a well after feeling thirsty.

One reason for untrustworthiness is not being able to take decisions. Such people are often in a dilemma thinking whether they should or shouldn't do a given thing, whether they should or shouldn't buy a particular item. Many a time they are in a fix, thinking, 'Why can't I take decisions? If I need to make a decision, should I consult someone or not? Why do I fear taking decisions?' Caught in such doubts, they avoid taking decisions.

If you fear taking decisions, it means you have not yet learnt the art of decision-making. Such a person fails to win the trust of others. If you do not have faith in your decision, first look at the options you have. Then begin with small decisions.

Don't worry if you take the wrong decision; it is important to take one. Gradually you will learn to take the right decision.

Listen to the suggestions of others, but do only what your heart feels is right. Listen to everyone but learn to decide for yourself. What usually happens is that we think for others and others think for us. We can take decisions for others very easily but when it's time to decide for ourselves, we take a long time.

Attachment towards our relations, our aspirations and our life make it difficult to arrive at a decision. You can learn the art of taking decisions by deciding to break attachments *(moh)*.

It seems very easy to decide for others but we feel scared to take even a calculated risk in deciding for ourselves. Actually, we are not aware of the fears present within us. Before taking decisions, we need to also win against our fears or eliminate them by taking small decisions at a time.

Numerous opportunities for taking decisions are coming your way every day. If you recognise every opportunity and learn to take advantage of it, then you will learn the art of taking right decisions and become dependable.

4. Cut out the escape routes of avoiding work

There are many in the world who want to do a lot many things but are unable to. Their lethargy, incomplete information and unconsciousness, which undermine the Foundation90, stop them from doing what they want to do.

If we have decided an aim of our life and if we want to achieve it, it is necessary that we acquire activeness, complete understanding and awareness. Cut out the escape routes available for escaping work and push aside the obstacles that come in the way of achieving your goal.

When courageous soldiers go into the battlefield, they like to hear the war cry: Do or die! For them, there is no possibility at all of running away from the battlefield. When they cross a bridge, they have only two options ahead of them – to win or to die. To cut out the escape route, they destroy the bridge after crossing it so that they do not have the option of escaping.

Use this technique in your life so as to become dependable. If you want to work on your health and gain fitness, then wake up early and join a gymnasium. Maybe you wake up late and miss out on exercise and thereby impair your health. In this situation, to make sure you exercise, go and pay the gym fees for an entire year. Those fees will push you into motion. You will then definitely get up early and go for exercise. This technique works for most people. If you are an exception, you can yourself easily look out for other techniques that cut out the escape routes. The intense desire of strengthening your Foundation90 will get you into the action mode.

'If one person in the world can do a particular thing, we too can do it.' On the basis of this understanding we always have to adopt an optimistic attitude.

5. Avoiding excuses, reinforce your strengths

People having a limp Foundation90 often give lame excuses and avoid work, as a result of which all their tasks remain incomplete. This not only harms them, but also troubles others.

A father said to his son at bedtime, 'Son, put out the lights.' The son replied, 'Dad, just close your eyes and think that the lights are out.' The father then said, 'Okay Son, just peek out of the window and tell me whether it is raining.' The son answered, 'Dad, the cat under your bed has just returned from outdoors. Touch it and see if it is wet.' Now the father said, 'Fine, won't you at least shut the door?'

The son said, 'Must I do all the work? Why don't you do some of it?!'

People who are indolent find various different excuses to avoid work. They feel that their excuses are proper, but before presenting any excuse, every one of us should ask ourselves, 'Is my excuse for not working right? Is it logical? Or am I avoiding work?' On doing this enquiry, we will come to know what kind of training we need to give ourselves. If we continue giving such response for every job, it will be very difficult to handle our character.

A person of character completes even difficult tasks without giving excuses in spite of facing several difficulties. If gold is heated in fire, it becomes all the more brilliant and fine. The more you heat it, the more it shines. Why does this happen? This happens because it has undergone repeated heating and it has endured so much. If you follow this example and decide on completing a given job without giving excuses, you too will shine through like gold.

To break away from excuses and reasons and get your body to work, realise the powers of your body. Make it robust and capable with the help of exercise and pranayam (breathing exercises). The sheer strength of a capable body can easily go through the rigours of any physical work.

To break away from excuses and reasons and get your body to work, train your mind so that your mental strength is enhanced. With intense mental strength, you can keep your mind unshakeable in the most difficult of situations. With high mental strength, you can easily carry out the most difficult of mental tasks.

To break away from excuses and reasons and get your body to work, purify your intellect so that your intellectual powers increase. With discriminative power and intelligence, you can take the most difficult of decisions in an instant. One, who lacks pure intellect, gives priority to excuses. With intellectual strength, man completes the main work of knowing his true self and performing self-enquiry honestly.

To break away from excuses and reasons and get your body to work, acquire spiritual knowledge so that your spiritual strength is reinforced. Spiritual strength helps man achieve the purpose of being born on Earth. Without spiritual strength, sympathy, compassion, non-violence and love are false. Spiritual strength can help defeat the inner demons of lust, anger, greed, attachment and ego.

Acquire all the strengths mentioned above. Carry out small experiments every day and become powerful. If you have to study something or need to complete some project and your mind is giving excuses, put up boards of 'No excuses please' wherever your eye goes frequently or wherever possible – at the study table, in the office, on your brush, in your car, on your wristwatch, etc.

In this way with a strong willpower, reinforce your physical strength, mental strength, intellectual strength and spiritual strength, in order to become a trustworthy and dependable person.

DAY 15

Improve Yourself

Handwriting and Reading Autobiographies

Tenth Remedy

A man's handwriting illustrates his character. The best way to improve our handwriting is to improve ourselves. This might sound strange, but it is true. Every person's handwriting says a lot about him. If you were to pay attention to people's handwriting, you can learn many things about them. During examinations, what did your handwriting look like when you wrote an answer you were unsure of? How did you write that word you were uncertain about? You try to create an impression of dual meaning from that word, so that it looks like one word as well as another. For the answer which you feel may be wrong, your handwriting also becomes constricted, unclear and ambiguous so that the examiner cannot understand what you have written. You can easily make out from the handwriting of a dishonest person that he is dishonest. Any person's state can be easily guessed from his handwriting.

Some people's handwriting tilts backward while that of some slants forward. This reveals whether the person lives in the fantasies of the future or in the passageways of the past. Some handwriting protrudes above the line, while some spills below the line. Several such finer nuances convey the mental state of the person.

When a person is undergoing transformation, he automatically sees a change in his handwriting. He sees that his handwriting is now improving. He is becoming straighter in his life. A frightened person's writing is constricted and a fearless person's writing is uninhibited. He is not afraid of what people might think, and writes with no inhibition. He has no fear. In this way, every form of handwriting tells about the nature of that person. Do not conclude that the person will always remain so. Self-transformation induces an improvement in handwriting and improvement in handwriting induces self-transformation.

A good way to improve handwriting is to write out a page every day. Make a daily effort to improve your handwriting. in this manner. Try to write like printed text. Or get a book on cursive handwriting from the market and practise writing on it. An even better approach is to improve yourself. When you get rid of the fears inside you, you will write in an uninhibited manner. Discipline will set in in your handwriting. You will feel a sparkle in your writing. This handwriting reflects your character and its beauty acts as a mirror to reflect the beauty of your character.

Seek inspiration by reading autobiographies

When you read the life-sketches and autobiographies of saints, you come to know their strong characters and learn how to boost your Foundation90. When you read the Buddha's book (character), observe what the cover (outer appearance) looked like and what the text (inner foundation) looked like. Similarly, if you were to read Mahavira's book, note the printed as well as the unprinted contents, and title of the book. Everything that is happening in your life happened in theirs too. But they always took positive steps even during those unpleasant events.

People who wish to augment their Foundation90, i.e., who wish to transform the contents published in their book into a beautiful text worth reading, must definitely read biographical sketches of great people. Reading about their high-quality characters inspires us to shape our characters as well. How many biographies have you read till date? As per your highest aim, do select some biographies and read them. You can realise its importance only after reading them. Life-sketches of some great men are given in the final section of this book.

By reading the life-sketches of every successful person of this world who has fortified his Foundation90 and worked continuously at it, you will get to know all these things. Some examples are Swami Vivekananda, the philosopher Socrates, freedom-fighters Lala Lajpat Rai and Bhagat Singh, poet and writer Ravindranath Tagore, Mahatma Gandhi, Dr. Babasaheb Ambedkar, Mother Teresa, Emperor Akbar, lady Muslim saint Rabiya, Saint Tukaram and other saints like him, Lord Rama's devotee Shabari, astronaut Kalpana Chawla, and many others.

All of these great men and women have risen to the heights of success as per their vision. Looking at their lives, you will learn what all they went through, the obstacles faced by them, and the faith with which they overcame every obstacle. They found a new and right way out of every difficulty. They had the faith that walking on that very path will consolidate their foundation and improve the life of others. Similarly, let unshakeable faith arise within you and let your autobiography become desirable for people to read too.

Four Steps to Fortify Your Foundation90

How to transform your negative energy

ELEVENTH REMEDY

We have all come to Earth with our own specific missions. Nature is always guiding us to accomplish that mission. If we have a sound character, we can walk unflinchingly and straight on the path shown by nature. Otherwise, with every small incident we will stumble and fall from this path due to getting trapped in greed, laziness and ignorance.

Whenever something positive, as per our mission, approaches us, we must be able to receive it in the right manner with an open mind. If you have prayed to nature: 'Please send to me whatever is mine, through the right course and in the right manner', then nature will respond that way to you. This prayer of yours itself symbolises the strength of your foundation. We will now learn of techniques that we can adopt to further fortify our Foundation90.

1. Do not become a slave and do not enslave others

A man of character neither succumbs to anybody nor tries to subdue anyone else. Due to being untrustworthy, people either succumb to others or exploit others. Those who get suppressed by others are definitely untrained people. In addition, those who try to enslave others are also untrained because they do not know that their work can get done without making a slave of others.

A key reason for the desire to enslave others is that every person wants his work to yield high output. The level of an individual's capability is inferred based on this output. Only after showing the outcome of their work, people get promoted.

People feel that the only way to accomplish their goal is to pressurise others so that their work can be finished on time. Those who succumb to this pressure are also untrained. They are unable to tell anyone openly what tasks they are capable of doing. They cannot clearly convey to the other person, 'Just entrust me with this responsibility. I will do the work.' Only when they are able to speak their hearts openly can they earn the trust of others and become self-reliant. A person who wants independence must think, 'I want to become independent. Whatever job I have undertaken, I should be able to do it on my own strength. I must gain expertise in my work to such an extent that looking at my work people should feel that it is no longer necessary to pressurise me.'

Some people acquire high positions without adequate training. Due to their higher ranks, they pressurise other people to get their jobs done because they want to show how capable they are. This is the only way they can show their capability. But they are unaware that their approach will result in them losing their position someday or remaining in the same position forever. Their company could freeze at the same point or sink down.

Ask yourself, 'What am I lacking due to which I am being pressurised or I am pressurising others?' Identify your shortcomings and get down to overcoming them. Do not sit and complain. Begin to work on your weak points. Even if this takes a year, it does not matter. If you start working from today, your purpose will be fulfilled in a year.

It is because of fear and greed that people either become slaves or enslave others. You have to work even if you feel scared. Let fear do its work. Fear is your body's feedback to you which tells you, 'You are about to do something new, something you have not done before.' It is such a good system that our body keeps a record of every work and conveys which work is being done for the first time, i.e. which job is new and which one has been done before. Thank your body for its feedback and tell yourself, 'I must do my work despite this fear.'

With new experiments, you have to now store new records (information) in your brain. On the next occasion, your body will say, 'You have done this work before. This is nothing new.

You can do this. You can handle this situation.' In this way, your self-confidence will go on mounting. Do not stop learning, no matter where you are, however high you have reached, because only learning can open new possibilities. First, you have to work on understanding what has already been created, and then prepare your body for what is yet to be created. This is a useful method to strengthen your Foundation90.

2. Stay balanced

You should always stay balanced with respect to health and circumstances. The body gets habituated to anything you train it for. If you habituate it to be lazy, the body begins to look for ways and means to escape from work. It constantly searches for excuses. Habituating the body towards laziness will decrease your ability for joyous self-expression (Expression of the Universal Self or God through your body). Hence, think which habit is useful for the future – to work or to not work? Do pay attention to your health.

Do not push yourself too much. Maintain balance between work and rest. Avoid both extremes. Rest before you get tired and work before you get lazy. When too much rest starts becoming a habit, then this habit goes on worsening gradually. You will notice in a year that lethargy in your body has increased much more than before. You are not able to work half as much as you used to. This habit will create problems for you in the future. Hence, at this time, train your body to work as much as possible. When you think of work as a burden, you will feel tired doing it. Then deceit seeps in to escape from work. Deceit destabilises the Foundation90. Therefore, do not think of work as a burden, instead think of it as a joyous form of self-expression.

3. Train yourself; learn to say 'No'

Always be prepared to train yourself. Do not miss any opportunity to provide training to yourself. Train your ears for what they must hear and what they must ignore. Train your eyes for which books to read and which to avoid. Stay away from that literature which shakes your foundation. Do not watch those programmes on television or the internet, which shake your foundation.

If you are not able to say 'No' for wrong things; if you are not able to tell, 'I cannot come with you, I cannot do this, please forgive me', then practise saying 'No' in front of a mirror. Repeat those lines many times standing before a mirror, which you want to tell people but are unable to, due to hesitation. Practise being honest and firm on your values, and reinforce your Foundation90.

4. Transform your energy and free yourself from vices

Energy is indestructible. It can neither be produced nor can it be destroyed; it can only be transformed. The vices such as lust, anger, greed, jealousy, etc. inside you can also be transformed. When you feel angry, if you box a sand-bag or if you work harder and more creatively at that time, then this energy gets transformed into creativity and your anger disappears.

When vices arise inside man, and when he defocuses his attention from those vices and performs meditation (or any spiritual practice, sadhana), then he redirects the energy expended in vices to Silence Meditation instead. Silence Meditation is also called as moun sadhana in which you experience the inner absolute silence. Some redirect this energy into creative activities and come up with new creations. In this way, the negative energy gets transformed. This energy helps in reinforcing your Foundation90. If you do not reorient the energies inside you correctly, these energies become the cause of debilitating your foundation and the building of your character collapses.

Mission Earth, knowledge of the highest truth, and the joy of devotion, can collectively help man to become free of vices. People often ask, 'How can we become free from vices? How can we fulfil our commitments? How can we become trustworthy?' The answer to all these questions is the same: 'Mission Earth, knowledge of Truth and joy of devotion.' Enhance these three aspects in your life.

More you remember the Mission Earth, stronger will your Foundation90 be. Due to incomplete knowledge, people are stuck in their weaknesses. With complete knowledge about life and life after death, man does only those actions that augment his Foundation90. If you are lacking in this knowledge, complete your knowledge through contemplation. When man finds the joy of devotion through complete knowledge, he automatically becomes free from illusory happiness of senses.

DAY 17

Contemplate on Religious Texts

Different texts, One message

TWELFTH REMEDY – DELVING INTO CONTEMPLATION

By God's amazing grace, the messages of the ultimate knowledge have reached Earth in the form of oracles. These messages from above are available for everyone in the form of religious texts. Some extracts from these religious texts are given below which can help you reinforce your Foundation90. Contemplate on these messages and commandments.

- **Useful instructions from Koran Majid to cultivate moral values**

  Seven taboos and forbidden deeds:

  - 1) Infanticide 2) Adultery 3) Unjustifiable murder 4) Looting orphans 5) Dishonesty in business (weigh properly, do not tamper with the balancing scales) 6) Believing fallacies 7) Display of ego

  - Drinking, gambling and false worship are all satanic acts. Stay away from these for your own good.

  - The good and the bad do not complement each other. It is better if you give goodness in return for the bad.

  - God is compassionate towards those who are compassionate towards everyone. Show compassion to the beings on Earth, and the one above will shower His compassion on you.

  - Assess before you speak. If the devil's provocation tickles your heart, seek refuge in God's abode.

  - Do not deliberately hide the truth. Do not mix the truth with lies. Always fulfil your promise.

  - Blaming your sin on an innocent is the greatest sin. Always give the true testimonial.

- **Instructions in the Bible by Moses and Jesus for building a virtuous character**

  - Blessed are those who do not follow the advice of immoral people. They are forever in the bliss of God's doings and witness His divine play.

  - The mind, intellect and focus of people with a bad character are engaged in misdeeds. Simplicity is a blessing. Deceit and bad behaviour are signs of lack of character.

  - Do not think bad, do not speak bad. Stay away from uttering devious words. Keep looking straight. Let your eyelids be open to what is before you. Walk on the path of the Truth and never stray away from this path.

God dislikes seven things:

1) Haughty eyes
2) A lying tongue (a dumb person is better than a talkative liar)
3) Hands that kill the innocent
4) A mind that thinks evil
5) Feet that race towards the wrong
6) A lying witness
7) A person who sows discord among brothers

- Beware of immoral women. Do not get caught up in their coercive sweet talk. Do not get influenced by their beauty or desire to attain them.

- Drinking liquor glorifies neither kings nor noblemen. It should not happen that they forget the rules while drunk and trespass over the rights of someone less fortunate.

☐ **Ten commandments of Moses:**

Moses received ten commandments from the Lord which are stated below:

1) Have no other gods before me…
2) Do not make an image or any likeliness of what is in the heavens above…
3) Do not take the name of God in vain…
4) Remember the Sabbath day and keep it holy…
5) Honour your father and your mother…
6) Do not kill…
7) Do not commit adultery…
8) Do not steal…
9) Do not bear false witness against your neighbour…
10) Do not covet your neighbour's house or anything that belongs to your neighbour…

☐ **Testaments of Guru Nanak and Guru Granth Sahib:**

1) Wear that kind of sacred thread (janeu) whose cotton is of compassion, whose yarn is of contentment, which bears the knot of self-restraint, whose twist is of truth, and which we can wear with a feeling of devotion. Just wearing it should enhance our devotion and inspire us to earn an honest living. Wearing it, we must live a deceit-free honest life... Only when we cultivate such qualities in us, have we truly worn the sacred thread.

2) If you wish to offer 'Namaz' five times, let the first Namaz be that of truth, the second of praise and prayer to God, the third of honest earnings, the fourth of giving for welfare of others and the fifth of purity of mind.

3) Rain falls the same everywhere, be it at heights or in the low-lying areas. But it accumulates more in the lower areas. Similarly, ego is something which is at a height; rain (grace of God) showers there too but cannot rest there.

4) Only if there is humanity and adequate virtues inside you, you will be welcomed in the court of God.

5) Purifying the mind, by itself is like going on Hajj (pilgrimage).

Contemplate on the Teachings of Saints

Several Saints, One message

THIRTEENTH REMEDY – CONTEMPLATION STATEMENT

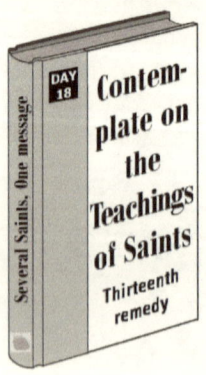

Till date, saints from several religions have guided people on how to fortify their character through their teachings, instructions, commandments, moral codes and principles. The guidance given by some of the saints is presented here.

The words in these teachings may appear to be different, but the underlying message in all is the same. Reading and contemplating on them will certainly benefit us in our lives.

❏ Five principles advocated by the Buddha (Panchsheel)

1) Not to lie and to always walk on the path of truth.

2) Not to take life (non-violence) and to never hurt any living being through your words, thoughts, feelings or actions.

3) Not to steal or consider others' possessions as your own.

4) Not to consume liquor or any other intoxicants and not to indulge in any vices such as gambling, etc.

5) Not to commit adultery, i.e. do not consider another's woman as your own and engage in sensual pleasures.

❏ Eight principles of Lord Mahavira

1) **Not to consume alcohol:** Not to consume anything that lowers man's level of awareness. In ignorance man consumes marijuana, opium and many such substances.

   Later on he becomes addicted to them. In his greed to easily attain the state of *samadhi**, he may give less importance to meditation and get caught up in intoxicants. Hence, in order to remain the master of oneself, Lord Mahavira has advised people to stay away from addictions.

2) **Not to consume meat:** Our mind is shaped by what we
*Samadhi: The state of consciousness before time began. Samadhi is a state which cannot be adequately described in words; it can only be experienced. It can be said that samadhi is being conscious of the true Self, transcending time and space. Or being in the state of undifferentiated beingness; a state of complete calm, tranquility and joy but where the mind

---

*Samadhi: The state of consciousness before time began. *Samadhi* is a state which cannot be adequately described in words; it can only be experienced. It can be said that Samadhi is the state of being conscious of the true Self, transcending time and space. Or being in the state of undifferentiated beingness; a state of complete alertness, tranquility and joy.

continues to be alert. eat. Consuming meat, cold and stale food increase the indolence of the body. Eating meat, fish and flesh of animals increases the tendency of violence in people. All the teachings of Lord Mahavira are based on nonviolence. One who loves every living being can alone become a devotee of non-violence.

3) **Non-violence:** Become sensitive and tolerant. Forgive every being and show them the way to attain liberation from misery. Promote brotherhood in the society by applying this rule.

4) **Not to become a slave to taste buds:** You must first control your tongue to acquire good health. The tongue must not become a slave of taste. The tongue must not use harsh words. Do not misuse the tongue to satisfy the greed for tasty food.

Using words inappropriately decreases the power of our words. Whatever words you use, similar kinds of thoughts are triggered in your mind. Remove abuse, bad-mouthing, sarcasm, bitching or lies from your words. Right use of the tongue is made by controlling the speech and the taste buds.

5) **Not to lie:** A person full of fraud, deceit and lies can never gather the courage to walk on the path of Truth. Man desires comfort by speaking lies. He wants to escape discipline and work by deceiving. He only wants to take by cheating others and escape from giving. He only wants to take from others. A man living on the principles of non-violence and love always wants to give. He never feels the need for any deceit.

6) **Not to steal:** This rule liberates man from greed. By keeping an eye on others' wealth, man brings harm to himself. Always keep an eye on others' knowledge, and not on their bodies or wealth. The one who disrupts others' spiritual practice or penance is also a thief. The one who steals always forgets his real mission. He remains captivated by the fear of being caught.

7) **Not to indulge in worldly and bodily pleasures:** Man believes himself to be the body, whereas he says, 'This is my body.' But

if this is 'my body', then how can I be the body? Just as my pillow cannot be me, my pen cannot be me, similarly my body cannot be me!

When we identify ourselves with our body, we indulge and get caught up in bodily pleasures. When man attains the Supreme Truth, he then wishes to use the body only for the expression of the Self, and not for worldly and sensual pleasures. This rule prepares man for the expression of the Supreme Truth through his body.

8) **Not to accumulate things:** Man cultivates a habit of accumulating everything because of his fear and greed. Because of this habit, he accumulates more than he needs. These very things hinder his journey on the path of Truth. Just as a traveller climbing a mountain goes on decreasing his baggage, similarly the Truth traveller goes on decreasing the accumulation of things. Manage with as little as possible.

❐ **Five *others'* to be avoided as preached by Saint Tukaram**

1) **Others' wealth:** You must not eye others' wealth. Saint Tukaram has referred to attraction to these others' as deep pits. Man falls into these pits and can then never reach the peak of the Truth.

2) **Others' women:** You must not think of someone else's woman. An incident had occurred with Saint Tukaram when he was in the mountains. A woman had come to him. What he said to her has appeared in one of his hymns. He told her, 'For me every woman is Mother Rakhumabai, just as Radha with Krishna is my mother.'

He who walks on the path of Truth decides on certain things in advance such as: 'I will not get involved in these issues.'

Saint Tukaram said that every woman is like his mother because he had already decided so. Hence, he was not worried to begin with. He further said to that lady, 'I cannot see your downfall. So please leave from here. Go to the village, go to the city, where you can find thousands of husbands. The entire world is full of such men.' Saint Tukaram's determination worked and that woman left.

3) **Criticism of others:** Beware of criticising others. There are two kinds of criticism. One is which you hand out to others. The other is which others hand out to you.

Saint Tukaram has said, 'Your critic's house should be next to yours.' This means that those who criticise and make fun of you should be your neighbours, just like Mumbaji was his neighbour. The hooligans of the village would always taunt him, and at home his wife would constantly rebuke him. He would be ridiculed frequently but he used these biting remarks for his inner selfdevelopment.

Criticism of others is a common bad habit in most people. They call others stupid or lazy. No sooner do some people come together than they start criticising about someone else saying, 'He is like this… She is like that… He must do this way… he must do that way…'

Beware of condemning others because this too is a dark pit. A person derives pleasure for a while by criticising others, but then he is unable to kick this habit. Hence, avoid criticism.

4) **Violence on others:** This includes causing pain to others or inflicting violence on others, which should be totally avoided as these tendencies take us down in the pits.

Our feelings, thoughts, words and actions should not harm any living being, animal, man, society, country or the world. If our feelings, thoughts, words or actions hurt someone, this is violence on our part. We should avoid it at least when we are fully conscious.

Unknowingly, our actions do harm others, but it should never happen knowingly.

5) **Respect from others:** This is also an 'other' we must stay away from. Man desires respect from others. Thereby he tries to grab others' attention. He becomes habituated and addicted to

getting appreciation from others and even does wrong things in order to gain praise. We must not get entangled in this.

Understand the one message from the different words used by saints. Keep your character unwavering through healthy and mature contemplation. Resolve to eliminate the eight causes that shake your Foundation90 and use the thirteen remedies to make it as strong as steel. You will then become rich with the wealth and strength of character. Do not misuse your Top10, but enhance its maturity. The second part of this book 'Top10' highlights this message.

When you do what you say,
when you say what you think,
and when you think what you feel,
then all the powers of nature
will come together to help you,
And you will become
integrated and trustworthy.

Do Not Consider Top10 to be Everything

Beware of cheap publicity

Many wrong notions about personality development have been firmly rooted in people. People consider the external appearance as complete personality.

Some people try to find fame only by decorating their Top10 (external appearance). Some people become famous by performing some crazy antics, which leads people to believe it to be an easy way to fame!

Top10 does not only comprise of your body, but also your speech and behaviour. It can prove dangerous when someone tries to impress people by the beauty of his physique, the apparent sweetness of his voice and the artificial softness of his behaviour, in order to fulfil his selfish desires. It is possible that such people get success in the beginning but soon their dishonesty will surface and the emptiness of their character would be revealed.

It is very difficult to gauge the depth of people's character by their external behaviour because people in fact do not behave as they actually are. There is a lot of dissonance between the reality and the behaviour of people. They do not appear as what they really are, and they try to show themselves as what they are not.

When students do not know the answer to some question during an examination, they often write it in such a handwriting that the examiner does not clearly understand what has been written, and the answer appears like this too and like that too. They do so in order to hide their ignorance.

Whenever you want to hide something, your handwriting becomes bad. If man's Foundation90 is fragile, how will his book be? It will obviously be written in bad handwriting.

Some people want to attain fame by indulging in destructive acts. There are instances of terror attacks which have led to a lot of destruction. With this, terrorist leaders who were not known before have become known to the entire world. Many others have got inspired by these leaders that they resort to similar acts. Such leaders are like books with impressive covers but completely hollow inside.

The paparazzi, impressed upon meeting these people, write how courageous and gracious they are. People get impressed because they cannot see their Foundation90. Only on the basis of their Top10, they make assumptions, which are wrong.

There are several self-proclaimed preachers even in the sphere of spiritualism who, in order to earn fame, have spread a lot of false beliefs in the name of spirituality. This only harms the interests of seekers of Truth who want to attain self-realisation. They get diverted from the path of Truth by hearing such beliefs.

The books of such individuals should be burnt in cool fire (i.e. the understanding of Truth) so that awareness is awakened among people.

If people get impressed by your outer personality, it is possible that in the future you may slide onto the path of deceit. Hence always be alert. If you know all these facts and become aware while there is still time, you will always be grateful to God for bestowing this grace upon you.

There have been many people in this world whose Top10 has been very powerful but their Foundation90 weak. The consequences of a shaky Foundation90 soon took a toll on their life in such a way that in no time their lofty world came crumbling down.

A person with an unstable Foundation90 does not hesitate from doing anything. This 'anything' could be lying, stealing, robbery, taking bribes or killing. Foundation90 never gets the chance to build and take root in those who are full of vices.

Therefore, the question of it falling to pieces does not even arise. Let us understand this aspect through the following examples.

1) Ravana

Ravana was the demon king in the famous Indian epic 'Ramayana'. Everyone is familiar with Ravana's Top10. People are occupied in decking their one face all their lives, and Ravana had ten faces! Ravana's Top10 was very impressive but his Foundation90 was slippery. He kidnapped Sita inspired by malice and lust, and so even today people burn his effigies.

People with weak character have hatred, envy and lust hidden inside them. When their character is revealed to the world, they are burnt to ashes. Ravana had to pay a hefty price for his weakness. He was totally annihilated.

2) Hitler

Hitler's example is known to all. He never got love from his parents in his childhood. Along with this, he also remained bereft of values of life. He had qualities and capabilities, his personality was magical and there was charisma in his outer appearance as well. But what can a man with fragile foundation give to the society? What did Hitler do? He placed innocent people in gas chambers and killed them. Children were lured into gas chambers, promising them games to play, and were mercilessly murdered.

3) Film artists

Some film artistes have adopted disrespectful and distasteful fashion to quickly rise up the popularity charts and become world famous. In order to make a name, such people only decorate their outer personality and adopt the wrong way by ensnaring people in this show biz.

People with unstable Foundation90 find pleasure in troubling others. Such people do become famous, but by wrong means. Just see how such people are remembered – people like Hitler, Mussolini, Tuglak, Stalin, Idi Amin, Osama bin Laden, Veerappan, etc. Even today, a strict officer, teacher or instructor is referred to as Hitler!

A weak Foundation90 gives rise to countless evils inside man, and day by day his level of consciousness goes on dipping. From the examples of such people, we get to learn that we must not weaken our Foundation90, rather we must try to consolidate it as much as possible. Only with a formidable Foundation90, we can accomplish the supreme goal of our life.

Among which books is your book placed?

What thoughts come to your mind on seeing the covers of the books shown below? Look at them carefully.

Now decide, what feelings should arise in people upon seeing you?

Do Not Misuse Your Top10

Unimpressive Top10 is also a grace

An *ashram* (hermitage) once had such a disciple who would lie a lot and incite clashes among other members. Everyone was troubled by him. One day, all the members of the ashram complained about him to the Guru. The Guru called the boy and told him, 'You must work on your Foundation90, i.e. your character.'

Hearing this, the disciple said, 'I am Unimpressive Top10 is also a grace not like that, I behave well with everyone. In fact these people are bad; they cannot tolerate my progress.'

Without any debate, the Guru said, 'Fine. If you are not like that, it's good.' After some days, the disciple was given proof of his bad character and he could not say anything in front of the Guru. He stood in shame.

'If you repeat the same in future, you will be expelled from the ashram,' he was ordered. When people argue to hide their shortcomings, they are serving their ego. To brighten your Foundation90, stop serving your ego. Some people do not want to contemplate honestly on their mistakes, even after they are told about it. Such people are given time and space to awaken and improve so that they too can restore their Foundation90.

Impressive Top10

Frail Foundation90 but excellent Top10 implies such people who are able to impress others with their personality but their foundation is feeble. Such people eventually get caught up in their own traps. They know how to please people with their personality, but due to a flimsy Foundation90, they continue to deceive people. People too get easily taken in by their charm. In this way they complicate situations. You would have seen such people around you too.

Those with a remarkable Top10 but vulnerable Foundation90 get quickly drawn towards wrong things. They become experts in duping people. However, eventually they end up harming themselves.

Due to their shallow Foundation90 such people misuse their impressive Top10 and spread wrong things in the society and take many others down along with themselves. Such individuals are very dangerous because people get easily charmed by their sweet talk and end up being ripped off.

These individuals use their outer personality time and again to attract people towards them. In schools and colleges, more often those students get trapped in bad habits who have a nice personality but are unaware about the importance of character. If children are not taught moral values in school and college, these children will take many others down along with them in the future.

Even a huge ship like Titanic sank because it saw only the top 10% of the glacier. The lower 90% of the glacier which is submerged inside the sea is not easily visible. You can perform a small experiment to understand this. Drop a cube of ice in a transparent glass filled with water and note what percentage of the ice is floating above the water surface and how much percentage is inside the water. You will find that 90% of the ice is inside the water and only 10% is visible above the water.

People form their opinions by seeing only the Top10. Titanic says, 'I am Titanic! I cannot sink.' Similarly, people develop an illusion about themselves and think, 'I am strong, I am not weak. It does not make any difference to me even if I do anything wrong.' This is exactly the ignorance that leads to downfall. Those who work only on their Top10 develop such kinds of delusions. History stands evidence that even big personalities like Titanic sink because of not being able to take care of their integrity. If such a thing can happen with a ship, then you can easily understand what can happen with us. We may have a ship of steel, but we should not think that despite the lack of integrity, nothing can touch us. Never get stuck in the illusion of outer personality.

Unimpressive Top10

People don't get taken in easily by those with an unimpressive Top10. Their personality does not impress people at once. However, they are told, 'It's not a bad thing that your personality does not impress people. In fact, you can take it as a kind of grace. Due to it you will not get quickly gravitated towards bad habits. Also, you will not get thoughts of fooling or swindling people and hence you will be able to work on your Foundation90 and always keep it sound.'

Best combination

Those with a good Top10 have to work on their Foundation90. The combination of best Foundation90 and best Top10 is the best combination. When both of these elements are strong, you will become a source of inspiration for others. If your Top10 is attractive, then people quickly accept what you say. But despite this, if you keep your integrity intact, then you are great. If you do not wish to steal money from others by lying and you do not want to deceive others, then this is a commendable thing. Those with a striking personality have to remain more alert. They are specially asked to work more on their Foundation90.

If your Top10 is impressive, then it is a grace only when you conjoin a sound Foundation90 with it, so that it becomes complete grace. Your life can then be fully dedicated towards service of the Truth and your book (autobiography) could be read for generations to come. If you wish, this is possible. This is your highest possibility. Until someone tells you your highest possibility, you do not break out of your comfort zone.

You can at the most think of what you want to become in your life. You cannot think more than that. But, do not limit your thinking because whenever you attain your decided goal, you will think that whatever you had thought was very limited. Right from today start building a solid Foundation90 in order to realise your full potential and do not let your Top10 become a curse.

DAY 21

Develop Maturity of Your Top10

Let your body language give out only one signal

When you got hurt by some object in your childhood, your parents hit that object. While hitting it, they said, 'This has hit you; now I will hit it.' This pleased you as a child and you laughed. At that moment your eyes were filled with tears and a smile appeared on your face. This is a usually adopted technique by parents to make a crying child laugh. The parents while hitting the object hold their hands and scream out pretending as if they have also been hurt by it. The child laughs even more on hearing its parents scream. It thinks, 'That object has been beaten up and my parents too got hurt; that means I am not the only one.' This diverts the child's attention elsewhere and it becomes quiet.

When you get hurt by some object after you have grown up, then your parents do not tell you, 'This object is bad. This has hit you, and so now I will hit it.' This is because after growing up, your physical strength and maturity increases.

If after growing up, the same things have to be done to please a person as were done during his childhood, then it is understood that he has not matured; to silence and please him, one has to hit some object. Thus, we should check and see what level of physical maturity have we attained.

When a child grows up, he understands that his body needs regular exercise and he always takes efforts for the same. He joins a good gym to remain physically fit. If he is overweight, he controls his body weight by working out in the gym and through diet control. If he is underweight, he makes a lot of effort to restore it to normal. Doing so, he gets a good feeling inside and experiences great health.

When you attain physical maturity, you understand your physical problems, if any. When your body needs medication, you provide it with medicines. In this way, you begin to understand and take care of your body. If you have not developed physical maturity, you cannot understand your physical problems. You wonder and you are confused whether your physical problem is due to lack of exercise or due to an illness for which you need to take medication.

Those who are involved in the spiritual practice of silence *(moun sadhana)*, and know *yoga* and *pranayam*, also know how to view physical problems. These practices also enhance our physical maturity and we go on becoming more and more mature.

Let your body language give out only one signal

If you have some pain or spasm in you body, ask yourself how long does such pain or spasm remain in your body? Is it permanent, temporary or keeps coming and going intermittently? Some people cry out loud upon feeling even the slightest of pain. Then the entire family consoles them and gives them all the attention. They feel good upon getting sympathy and attention. When someone screams just in order to draw people's attention towards him, it means that this person has grown up physically but has not developed physical maturity.

If people get a wrong message looking at your body, your expressions and your behaviour, then you have not yet gained physical maturity. If you do not know that your body is giving out wrong messages or signals, you have not become mature as yet.

Many people are not aware of what facial expressions appear on their face when they are listening to someone. If a person's facial expressions do not correlate with his internal feelings, it means he has not yet learnt body language. If your facial expressions convey to the person conversing with you that everything he has been saying is utter nonsense, then that person will feel confused, thinking, 'Should I say anything further to this man or not, should I give him the message or not?'

What does our face tell people? What do our facial expressions and body language tell people? Let us correctly transmit this language. Let us not give two messages at the same time. If you want to say one thing to a person, then let only one message or signal reach him, not two. Your message should not appear as a 'yes' and a 'no' together. Just as in movies the actor and the co-actor both feel that the actress is interested in marrying him. The actress's behaviour is creating confusion in people; it implies that she has not attained physical maturity. In this way, lack of physical maturity gives birth to a lot of misunderstandings and conflicts.

The signal transmitted by your body language must be devoid of any confusion. People should understand what your aim is and what you wish for in your life. You should yourself decide what your life (book) must be like. When you are able to decide your goal, then dualistic signals will never be transmitted by you.

When people go for parties and someone offers them a drink, they say 'no' in such a way that their 'no' can at any point turn to a 'yes'. Such people quickly fall into the trap of addictions because they are never able to decide what they should do in life and which path to walk on. Physical maturity is delayed in such people.

Sometimes our face displays hatred, sometimes anger and sometimes love. That is why people cannot understand us and what we want. Hence, we must enhance our physical maturity.

Just because our bodies have grown up, it does not mean that we have grown up. If we have developed physical, mental, social, financial and spiritual maturity, only then we have truly grown up. In order to attain such maturity, we must first work on our body language. When our body language conveys the right message to others, very soon we will find that our body (Top10) is transmitting the highest consciousness (experience of the 'Hidden Zero'). The next part of the book is dedicated towards manifestation of this Hidden Infinity or Hidden Zero. Without the Hidden Zero, Foundation90 and Top10 are like a corpse, which come alive when 'Zero' associates with them.

*Incomplete actions give
birth to excuses.
Excuses give birth to lies.
Repeated lies give birth to
wrong tendencies.
And wrong tendencies give
birth to a bad character*

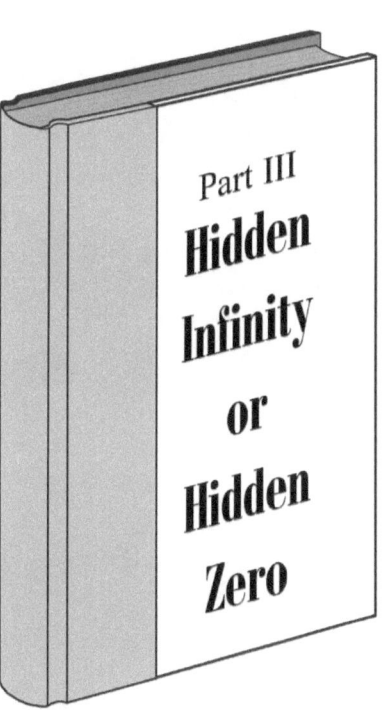

Living in Zero is the Reality

$90+10+0 = 100\%$

The 'Zero' being referred to here is the same as infinity. It represents the infinite Universal Self present within us, which is also called as 'nothingness' and hence 'Zero'. Leading life while remaining in Zero is the reality. And reality is the same for everyone. Can there be such a person, who is using something about which he knows nothing and is not even interested in knowing 90+10+0=100% about it? Let us understand this with an example.

When you are using a pen, you would want to know how the pen works, how many refills are inside it, one or four? You would want to know all the potential possibilities of that pen. Supposing, it had four refills, and you had been writing with it all your life thinking it had only one refill. In the end when this reality strikes you, you would say, 'Had someone told me earlier that this pen had four refills of different colours, I would have made full use of the pen.'

Similarly, the Hidden Zero tells you: What is the highest possibility of this body you have received? What all has been placed inside this body? Which treasure is hidden inside it? In Zero or Infinity, you are reminded of that treasure. Knowing this Infinity is not for some special people; it is for all. Every person must know what all is possible through the body that he has got. When people bring home something new, some new machine or appliance, they first read its instruction manual. They read it so that they have full information about the equipment they are about to use.

Likewise, you should have complete information about the body that you are going to use. How are its Foundation90 and Top10 like? *Who* has got this body? True spirituality (knowledge of Zero) gives you this information, and is therefore essential for all. Some people think that spirituality is for those who are in trouble or who want to run away from life or who cannot fight the battle of life. These are all wrong notions; discard them from your mind.

You go to school and college for fifteen years or more. Does this mean you were running away from your life for fifteen years? No. It does not mean so. The purpose is to make a career (a source of livelihood) after your studies, to become a doctor, an engineer or something else. This is not running away from home. This is preparation to return home. After setting your career, you return home fully prepared. If someone were to think of not returning from the college, and to sit there always, then this would be running away from life.

Knowledge of Zero is also for those who wish to become instrumental for the world to become a better place and to serve humanity in the right manner. Many want to help others. They have the feeling of service inside them. They render service out of love. Therefore, they wish to have the knowledge of Zero, which not only benefits them personally but also fulfils their purpose.

When the thought appeared in the Buddha's mind that there is nothing but misery and sorrow, he set out from his home in search of the Zero. That sorrow became a source of inspiration for Buddha. He succeeded to overcome his sorrow and also became a source of inspiration for many others to permanently get rid of sorrow.

Some people venture into spirituality to acquire the right knowledge and understanding because they wish to know a better technique to use everything. They enter spirituality to learn a new way of living life. Some are in love with God and so they are ready to become Zero. They always wish to sing praises of the world created by God.

Decide, according to the title of your book, the importance of Zero in your life, and how essential it is to understand the experience of Zero, which is hidden inside all of us.

Foundation90 + Top10 + Hidden0 = 100% Complete Aim

DAY 23

Zero Experience is Beyond Inside and Outside

Free Sample

Zero experience or experience of the infinite is permanent. It is neither inside nor outside. It is beyond inside and outside. To know the Zero experience is to know oneself. We cannot get this Zero experience somewhere outside, it is in fact hidden inside us. Zero Experience means our existence, our being, the Truth,

God, Self, Supreme Bliss, the 'Nothing' that has the potential for everything. Free sample

Unless and until one recognises the Zero experience, questions arise in the mind whether this Experience of Being exists outside the body or inside? Is the experience felt because of the body or is it felt on the body? Only examples can be given to understand this:

1) 'Is the syrup present inside the *rasgullas* (sweet balls soaked in sugary syrup) or also outside them?' You would say, 'The *rasgulla* is within the syrup. There is syrup inside it as well as outside.' Similarly, the Zero experience is inside as well as outside.

2) A fish lives inside water and is surrounded on all sides by water. It lives within the water. It could keep searching for water and not find it because the water is so close to its eyes and stuck to it that it does not even realise that it is inside water. In the same way, the Zero Experience is so close to us that we do not realise if it is inside us or we are inside it. In fact, Zero experience surrounds us on all sides.

3) Just as you deep fry *bhajiyas* (Indian fried dish) in oil, similarly all bodies have appeared in this world which is filled with Zero experience. This experience is inside each body as well as outside, just as oil is inside the *bhajiyas* and also outside them.

You cannot recognise the Hidden Zero or Infinite experience with your mind. Even if Hidden Infinity stands right in front of the mind, the mind cannot recognise it because it has presumed and imagined it to be something else. Like, you have ordered for doughnuts in a restaurant, and if squareshaped blue-coloured doughnuts were placed before you, you will ignore them even after seeing them, because you have never seen square blue doughnuts before. You have always seen doughnuts that were ring shaped, and never of any other shape. You will sit waiting for your order of ring-shaped doughnuts to arrive, whereas your order has arrived long back.

In the same way, the Hidden Zero experience is always with you. You only need to attain the understanding of how to know it.

Understanding Zero experience with the intellect is the first step. After understanding it through the intellect, you will also understand it by self-experience. For instance, one has learnt the alphabets from A to Z, but says, 'I have learnt all the alphabets, but I don't know how to form words.' You would tell him, 'Since you have learnt the alphabets, you will also learn to form words.'

If you have understood Zero experience with your intellect, it will begin to manifest in your life. You would then question yourself in every incident, 'What am I considering myself as in this incident…? What do I believe myself to be when taking this decision…? Am I thinking myself to be the body…?' When you remember this again and again, then the bliss of Zero will begin to get down at the experiential level too.

In order to understand the Hidden Zero experience in all its completeness, keep on performing self-enquiry with understanding. Enquire about yourself in every event. Whenever you feel anger, hatred, boredom, fear, ego or greed, ask yourself, 'To whom has this anger appeared and what exactly is happening to me in anger?'… 'When do I get bored and why does my body need excitement?'… 'Which underlying belief of mine is working behind my fear? … What kind of happiness is my greed providing me with?' … 'Who is the one who actually possesses this ego?'… 'Who am I?'

In order to stabilise in the Zero experience, sit in silence every day and ask yourself, 'Who am I?' This question will take you to your inner depths, which will enable you to know your actual nature, your 'beingness', which is being referred to as the Hidden Infinity or Hidden Zero.

Nature gives man the experience of the Hidden Zero (the Truth) every morning, in the form of a sample. Every salesman who sells a product offers a small free sample of that product so that the consumer can get a little taste of what it's like. Similarly, Nature also offers every man a free sample of the Zero experience every morning so that man gets a taste of that experience. However, upon waking up in the morning, man immediately remembers all his various chores and tasks, and therefore misses the free sample. The first thought that occurs to a person upon waking up is, 'What do I have to do today? Which jobs are pending?' In the whirlpool of these thoughts, he misses the free sample.

Perform this little experiment every morning. If you wake up at 6, tell yourself that you woke up at 6:15. Then in those fifteen minutes between 6 and 6:15, sit quiet and feel the Zero experience. Consider that you woke up at 6:15, otherwise as soon as you get up at 6, immediately thoughts rush in such as: 'What all tasks do I have to do today? Which places do I have to go? Which meetings do I have today? I have to do this… I have to do that… breakfast is to be prepared…' At such times, ask yourself what would have happened had you woken up at 6:15 instead? In those fifteen minutes, try to take advantage of the free sample of Truth Experience that nature is offering us. On awakening in the morning, you are very close to the Zero experience and so it is easy to go onto that experience at that time with awareness.

When you sit in silence during the evening after the entire day's work, you are very far from Zero experience. After sitting in silence, you first get to see the thoughts of your entire day, and only after that does the Zero experience manifest. Whereas every morning, nature gives you this experience so easily. By feeling this experience in this way every morning, within a few months you will be able to feel the Infinity or Zero experience at any point of time in the day. All decisions are taken correctly only from this Zero experience and life becomes truly successful and complete.

Foundation90 + Top10 + Hidden0 = 100%

Two Aspects of Understanding Zero

The Self Experience Truth

Alexander was once asked by a great saint, 'What would you do after conquering the world?'

Alexander very proudly replied, 'I will establish my command over the entire world.'

The saint then asked, 'What will you do after establishing your command over the entire world?'

Alexander fell silent on hearing this The Self Experience Truth question. He was stunned and started thinking, 'What would I do after I have my established my domination over the entire world?' This was a difficult question that appeared before Alexander, because after conquering the whole world, the zeal and energy inside him would not find any opportunity for expression. What would he do after having captured everything? This question had never occurred to him before. When someone forced him to reflect on this question, he felt sad. By taking this question in the right manner, he could have reached the Hidden Infinite experience, where there is neither sorrow nor dissatisfaction, only contentment and fulfilment. But this did not happen due to Alexander's 'unbright' or personal ambitions.

When man thinks what he would do after all his work is done, he feels tensed and depressed. Due to incomplete contemplation, a sense of dissatisfaction begins. Then, man starts thinking something new and he begins to see things in a new way. This means that after complete contemplation, he gets a new Truth Vision. On attaining this Truth vision, he takes steps towards contentment.

First aspect of Zero – Experience of Self

When thirst arises inside man to know the Hidden Zero experience, he wishes to remain with the Truth, merge in the Truth and become the Truth. He thinks, 'If these particular factors are hindering me from remaining with the Truth, let me start getting rid of these factors right now. What should I do so as to completely get rid of all wrong and negative habits and tendencies?'

When man contemplates constantly, conviction develops inside him. He then resolves: 'I am not going to get involved in anything that will take me away from the Truth.' At the first step, conviction arises in man and then he takes a firm decision based on this conviction.

After the first step, the second step arises from the Zero or Infinite Experience. Then there is no need to check whether it is right or not. Since it arises out of the Experience, it has to be right. From the external appearance, people may feel that things are going wrong, but actually they are right. Without the Experience, man may appear to be taking the right step, but it is proved to be wrong because it has not arisen out of the Zero experience.

Every step arising from the Zero experience has arisen from the depths of devotion. It is very apparent there how many people are going to benefit from this action. It could appear as if something wrong is being done towards some people, or the interests of some people are being harmed. But from the place where this decision arose and the understanding with which this decision was taken, it is very clear that this very action is going to bring about the welfare of people. It was essential to take this action.

Only after reaching the heights of consciousness, man finds such determination. In order that people should be able to understand this step, the Hidden Zero or Infinity must be talked about. They should be told, 'This is Experience of Self, which is your 'being', your 'presence'. You are not the body, but due to the body you are able to feel your Self. If you are able to see this clearly, find out: Why are you connected with this body? What are you doing with this body? Are you doing that which you were supposed to do on associating with this body?'

By developing attachment with the body and becoming identified with it, man forgets his actual aim and gets engrossed in his personal aspirations. Every action of ours must arise from the Zero experience because our every action tells us who we actually are. Man's thoughts reflect what he is considering himself as. If he is leading his life thinking of himself as the body, this is ignorance. All the thoughts that appear in us from morning till night, are informing us about us and our ignorance.

Step from dissatisfaction towards satisfaction

If you were to think by being on the Hidden Zero experience, i.e. by being who you actually are, there would be no dissatisfaction as felt by Alexander. Then, such thoughts do not occur to man: 'Nothing great happened in my life. I do not feel so good or special. What will happen after I die? I will not be able to see the fruit of the seeds I have sown, then what is the point?' After knowing one's true self, man becomes free from such kinds of negative thoughts. He leads his life being what he really is.

Man always remains miserable in ignorance. Due to ignorance, he is not able to participate in any grand beneficiary cause. With his limited intellect, he thinks, 'What is the use of doing such work which will take hundred years to complete. I will not even be there at that time.' Such thinking limits man from doing something big. But if one sees with understanding and from the Zero experience, then every thing and every incident becomes an opportunity that gives completeness to life. Man is never able to take any new step with negative thinking. Therefore, the intellect must always be fed with positive thoughts. Even the act of sowing seeds of positive thoughts takes you towards the Hidden Zero because nature is always positive.

Let us use the body by being who we are

Some people are able to take new steps in their life because they are able to remain in the Zero experience and take decisions by being in that experience. Whenever they are on the Zero experience, they can clearly see which things have become hazy due to which we are going further away from our mission. When man forgets the purpose of his life, he remains engaged in the whims of his mind. He is then constantly reminded of his real aim and told, 'You are not the body. You are experiencing yourself through this body. The essence of life flows through you. You are feeling yourself to be alive. This is that experience, by being on which you become unlimited and are able to think being unlimited.'

The body which we have received must be used for realising the highest goal; otherwise man forgets using the body for his goal and uses it for everything else instead. You know how to use a mike and you also know its importance. If someone were to use a mike as a hammer, you would tell him, 'This is wrong use of a mike. The mike can be used for better purposes.' Same is the case with man's body. Unlimited thoughts of the highest order can appear through the body. Such a thought can emerge which has never appeared before in any body in the world. If such a thought is not appearing in our body today, it indicates that we do not know of the Infinity experience. We are merely considering ourselves as the body. When we begin to feel the experience of 'being' inside us, then we will start using the body being who we actually are.

When such state arises, the feeling of 'false I' is no longer there. We no more think that 'this thought has come from my body'. The understanding in that state is, 'The thought may have come from any body, but I know that this thought has originated from the Zero or Infinity region.'

When you will know the answer to the question 'Who am I?' at the experiential level, then the dust of illusion that has gathered on the Zero experience will get cleared. The more we listen about the Zero experience and contemplate on it, the more we will find it new every time. You will feel as if you have met yourself for the first time. Every time we meet the Zero experience for the first time. Then everyone appears to be new, bright and fresh to us. Stabilisation on the Zero experience is such a state, being on which no one feels bored, on the contrary he always feels fresh and blissful.

Second Aspect of Zero – The Truth

Every thing belonging to the mind's arena does feel boring at some point or the other; the mind gets fed up with the same thing. However, when the mind falls in love with the Truth, it surrenders completely. It even gets ready to die in Bright Love for the Truth. Stabilisation in the Truth means the death of the judging mind. If we are feeling bored being with the Truth, it implies that we have not yet known the Truth. We do catch glimpses of that Zero experience at times during the day, but it gets blurred after a while.

Man sees light in his body, feels sensations on his body and also feels the powers of the chakras, but these are not the Truth. All of these things can facilitate one in attaining the Truth, but they themselves are not the Truth. Each of these has its own benefits. We have to, in fact, understand this body-mind mechanism, on which the sensations arise and which acquires power from the chakras (energy vortices in the body). But if you consider these things to be the Truth, you would be under an illusion. Expression of the Truth can take place through the body. We have to, at every instant, use our body only for expression of the Truth. For this, we have to ask ourselves,

'What things are lacking in my body for the expression of the Truth? Which qualities must I cultivate? Which is the language that I do not know but I must learn, which can help in the highest expression of the Truth through my body? Which skills should I develop so that this body becomes instrumental for the Truth? What are the vices in my body that are blocking the expression of the Truth?' By asking yourself such questions and by making your body virtuous, you will very soon get stabilised in the Zero or Infinity experience.

90+10+0 = 100%

Enhance Your Spiritual Maturity

Maturity in Inner Silence

The most important facet of life is 'spiritual maturity'. When man treads the path of spirituality, he does not know what he is going to get by walking this path. He enters the realm of spirituality on people's suggestion and then understands how and why to practise meditation and silence. Practising silence bears its own fruits and gives rise to joy. The feeling of the body disappears Maturity in Moun (Silence) in the state of silence. The next time he meditates, he constantly gets thoughts such as, 'Why am I still not feeling that joy… why isn't the sensation of body disappearing… I am not getting the same experience as the last time… ' In this way, based on his presumptions he keeps checking if he is getting the same experience. When this happens with you, tell yourself, 'I have not yet attained spiritual maturity.' People are unable to mature because of not getting guidance from an appropriate master on a subject such as spirituality.

Do not get entangled in results

Once upon a time, some devotees with the feeling of devotional service began creating an ashram (hermitage). After some time, it was observed that they were getting more involved in the results thinking, 'Why is this person taking over my role? This was my job, why did he do it? Why is he taking a share in my credit? Why do people run after credit? I have done most of the work, but someone else gets the credit… '

When people had begun with this service, these were not the feelings inside them. They felt happy simply in rendering service but later when some were awarded, the rest thought, 'Next time, we too shall get an award.' And when they did not receive any awards, they started feeling bad. Such people, by giving more importance to outcome (fruit) rather than their deeds (karma), remain spiritually immature.

Similarly, when a person begins to practise meditation, he feels the benefits after some sessions (in the form of getting the Zero experience). After seeing this result, now he meditates to get that result. The first time when he sat down to meditate, was it for these benefits? No. He started to meditate with the thought that it is a good practice. Then after some days of practising meditation, he starts feeling refreshed and happy. Now he thinks, 'Why don't I feel this way always?' He gets entangled in results.

While travelling by road, you see milestones on the way. These milestones indicate how far your destination is from you: there are 6 km more to go, 5 km or 4 km… Seeing them, you understand that these are milestones which one encounters frequently while travelling, and you continue further. You never think, 'These are beautiful stones,' and stay back. You do not end your journey and sit on those stones with an umbrella thinking, 'This place feels good' or 'This is a good sight.' You move ahead in your journey.

Likewise, while practising meditation, you should not get stuck in its benefits. You will get various experiences through meditation – you will feel lightness of your body, your concentration will improve, your willpower will increase, and there will be many other benefits. But remember that in order to get the experience of Zero *(samadhi)* and to stabilise in the Zero experience, these are only milestones on the path of meditation, and not the destination itself. You must not stop at the various physical experiences but continue your practice.

Be a witness and see

If yesterday you had felt refreshed during meditation, that was yesterday's state. If this is not your state today, then you must understand that yesterday's state is now a thing of the past. In today's practice, you will encounter a newer state; be prepared to see that state. Do not harbour the desire in your mind to re-experience past states. If that state recurs, it is fine. Think of it as grace when you get any experience but always remember that you do not practise meditation for these experiences. This grace is bestowed so that you develop the conviction that you are not the body. Understand that you get these experiences only to tell you that you are not the body. Do not sit with any presumptions while practising meditation and wonder, 'Why this is not happening… why am I not feeling light… why are my legs feeling numb… this did not happen yesterday, why is it happening today…?' Even if you feel this way, tell yourself that yesterday's state was different and today's state will be different. See what happens today. Be a witness and watch with detachment so that you can perceive the Self Witness (Zero experience). This is spiritual maturity.

Always remember the primary purpose

Suppose one day you have to prepare dinner for twenty people. You go to the market to buy vegetables accordingly. You find that some vegetables are being sold free of cost. In such a situation, you must first buy those vegetables which you had come to buy. If, getting engrossed in the free bonanza, you forget to buy the main vegetable that you had come for, then it is possible that that vegetable is no longer available when you finally remember it. You would surely bring home free vegetables, but you did not find enough of that vegetable which you had really wanted to prepare for your guests.

Similarly, when you meditate, are you attaining the understanding that you should have been? Are you buying the vegetable (conviction) that you should be buying? Or are you getting stuck in free vegetables (other experiences or benefits)? This does not mean that you should not take free items. Do take them, but first take the most important one. The most important or primary message is that you must gain conviction through meditation that you are not the body. Know this through your experience.

Every thought is a prayer

Are you receiving what is being given through meditation – the Supreme Truth? Why do we go into the state of meditation? What happens in that waiting period? The fact is that in that period, all our prayers are getting answered. If we have prayed, after that we must also remain silent for some time so that our prayers can be worked upon.

When you go to a restaurant and order for something, you then wait for the order to arrive. If you do not remain quiet during this period, and keep holding the waiter telling him something again and again, how can he get your order? When the waiter begins to leave to get your order, you call him and say, 'Wait, do not get this vegetable. Instead get the other one.' And when he begins to leave, again you call him, 'Hey, wait! Come here for a minute. Tell me what is there for salad?' If you do this all the time, when will food arrive on your table? When will you start eating?

Same is the case with meditation. After sitting in meditation if you keep thinking repeatedly, 'When will I feel that experience…? When will my thoughts stop…?', then you will be told to sit quietly without anticipating any experience. Give the order to the waiter (nature) and let it work on it. The results will come automatically.

Man thinks from morning to night. These thoughts are actually his prayers. He is unaware of this. Every moment, prayers arise in him. This means, with so many prayers, he also has to sit quiet for some time during the day. When you sit with eyes closed, thoughts do not stop at once on closing your eyes. Some person can place orders to the waiter even with closed eyes, 'Ok, listen, do you have mushrooms? Do you have Chinese dishes?' He continues to speak with closed eyes. In the same way, you will notice that even with eyes closed during meditation, thoughts continue for some time. There is no problem in this, but your job is that you have to sit quietly for some time. Subsequently, you will begin to watch your thoughts in a detached manner. Slowly, the pace of thoughts will decrease and the gap between two thoughts will increase. Whether this gap widens or not, you should not get stuck in results. Your job is to sit. Let us give ourselves the opportunity to sit in meditation*, so that the prayers we are offering can be answered.

When you attain maturity right from the physical aspect to the spiritual aspect, you will be able to say, 'Now, I am fully mature and developed. Now I know what is to be done while sitting in silence.' The conviction that 'I am not the body' gained through silence should be maintained forever and not forgotten. It should not happen that after coming out from meditation, you forget why you meditated or what was your purpose behind meditation.

Attain conviction through silence

After going into silence, you develop the conviction that 'I am not the body.' After coming out of silence, you have to see whether this conviction manifests in your behaviour as well.

---

*To know more about meditation and meditation techniques, you can read the book 'You are Meditation' by Sirshree..

If you overeat after coming out of silence, because the food was delicious, then you should understand that you still lack conviction.

Eat only as much is needed by the body to function. If you eat more than what is required, your body will not be able to help you in your efforts to attain your ultimate goal. This is your responsibility and not your body's. The body can only indicate if the food is tasty or not. Your body is a great friend of yours. It provides you constant feedback but it is your duty to decide how much to feed it. If you feed it more than needed, this indicates less maturity on your side. If you do not correctly use the maturity that you earned in silence, it means that you did not gain anything from such Silence Meditation.

Do not change your decisions looking at the present scene

You have to attain maturity in all five domains of life – physical, mental, financial, social and spiritual. If you attain spiritual maturity, you will find that other domains of your life will automatically benefit. You would then not forget your mission of life by getting influenced by the present scenes.

Let us understand what is meant by 'the present scene'. Say, a man steps outside his house to buy something and he meets a friend on the way. He then forgets why he had set out in the first place. This means that an incident of the present took over him. What would you do if you decide something, and then suddenly the scene changes? Will your decision change? If this is happening with you, you have not yet fully matured.

You had been thinking of sitting to meditate. Just then someone comes to the room and puts on the television. You change your mind thinking, 'Let me watch the television now. I will meditate later.' This means that our decisions change by change in the scene.

We must reflect over who is guiding us. Is our understanding guiding us or the scene in front of us, the voices around us, the alluring fragrance, the captivating surroundings or the seductive touch? The right factors should guide us so that we do what we have decided to do through contemplation. Maha Nirvan Nirmaan (highest expression of the Self) requires unshakeable body-mind mechanisms. They must remain undeterred from their mission even when the scene changes.

Only those who wish to work at the highest level of consciousness will be available to create Maha Nirvan Nirmaan. Otherwise as the scenes in front of them change, immature people will keep oscillating to and fro.

You have to attain spiritual maturity, so that this does not happen with you. When you sit for Silence Meditation, make a firm resolution: 'I will not stop practising silence, whether I get any experience or not.' When you sit in silence with this determination, you are giving God an opportunity to help you hundred percent.

Ninety + Ten + Zero = Good fortune, Blessing of God,

Hundred percent

Epitome of Self-Development

Mahatma Gandhi

With a mission, knowledge and love, what heights of self development man can reach – this is depicted by the life of Mahatma Gandhi. Till date several books have been written on Gandhiji's life and character. On learning about his character, you will be able to glance into your own life and understand how to shape your own character.

Gandhiji's life started as that of a common man but he learnt something from every incident, and improved upon all his mistakes. Gradually he transformed from a common man to a great soul.

Right from childhood, Gandhiji encountered several problems. He was of a shy and timid nature. He used to always think that snakes would emerge from one direction, dacoits would attack from the other direction, ghosts would appear from the third direction, and 'what would people say' from the fourth direction. He was unable to sleep at night without having the lights on. He was a below-average student in his class. If an average student scores ordinary marks just enough to pass, Gandhiji scored even lesser.

These things about Gandhiji are being told to you so that you are able to see the possibility of your progress. You will definitely feel inspired by reading the life-sketch of Gandhiji. If you lack certain qualities, it does not mean that you cannot progress in your life or that you cannot become a person of character. Rather you must think what was there in Gandhiji that made him the Father of the Nation. You can compare his life with yours: Are the obstacles in your life more than the ones in his life or are they lesser?

The main reason for Gandhiji's popularity is his principles. These very principles inspired him to undertake noble work. He did not just speak about great work, but actually made it happen. He was trustworthy because there was no discrepancy between his words and his actions.

Gandhiji got married at the young age of 13. The understanding that is attained after maturity was absent in him at that age. He even tried to be a doctor but was unsuccessful. Then, on his uncle's suggestion, he left for London to study law.

Before leaving for London, his mother had told him to always eat vegetarian food and to stay away from meat. Due to this his health deteriorated further. He had to struggle a lot to find vegetarian food abroad. He had to walk on foot for long distances in search of veg food, which proved to be a preparation for his Dandi March in the future. Even at a ripe age he was able to walk very fast and cover long distances so easily that people would be surprised at how he could walk so much even in his old age!

From this incident, one can also learn that Gandhiji kept his promises. He had promised his mother, but even if he were to consume meat abroad, his mother could not have known about it. Yet, he did not do so. Fulfilling promises was one of his many virtues, which is an important quality that every man of character should possess.

While in London, Gandhiji initially feared that the white people may consider him uncultured and a lowly villager. Thinking so, he brought a change in his wardrobe. He got new clothes for himself, bought a new hat, got a new haircut, learnt to wear a tie, and bought a watch with a golden chain. He wanted to be part of the cultured society, and so he bought a violin, learnt the French language and also learnt to dance. But soon he understood that all these things were meaningless.

Gandhiji was an honest thinker. This was a very important and great quality he possessed. If this quality of his were to be imbibed by everyone, it wouldn't take long for everyone to become virtuous. At that time, Gandhiji thought honestly, 'What would be the right thing to do in this situation? I have changed my dressing. I have changed my lifestyle. But have I changed from inside with these external changes?' When a person converses with himself honestly, he does get the right answer. The answer that emerged within Gandhiji was, 'You are still the same from inside… you are still afraid thinking "what will others say?" Do you have to do such things only because you see such kind of people around?… ' He then gave up all those things. He sold off his violin. He understood that by working on the outer appearance (straightening the Top10), no one can achieve internal beauty. He, whose foundation is firm and whose character is pure, does not get stuck in external appearances.

Gandhiji possessed the unfailing weapon of non-violence. With this weapon, he convincingly defeated the British Army, which was the best and the most powerful army in the world. It was the principles founded on Gandhiji's non-violence that liberated India from the clutches of slavery.

The historian Mr. Kripalani once told Gandhiji, 'You have chosen such a way to get rid of the British which is never going to yield any results. History is proof that no one has been able to achieve victory through non-violence.' Gandhiji replied, 'Perhaps you do not know history very well... Is it written in history that what has not happened till date will never happen in the future? In fact, history is made when someone takes a new step!'

Gandhiji used to say, 'He, who has chosen non-violence with all his heart and soul, has such power that no one in this world can match.' Non-violence means love and fearlessness. Where non-violence rules, there is fearlessness and no insecurity. Otherwise there is always a fear that the opposite person would shout at us, or raise his hand and hit us, and in that situation we will not be able to follow non-violence. Due to this fear, you would want to hit the other person first. Before he raises his hand to hit, you would want to hit him. That is why we have to understand the real meaning of nonviolence.

Once, Gandhiji was pleading a case in the court and his legs were trembling out of fear. He handed over the case mid-way to his friend, saying, 'You take over from here.' People laughed at him a lot at that time. He felt very humiliated and dejected. Till the time he worked for himself, he never felt selfconfident. However, when he started fighting for others, he was filled with self-confidence. He spoke for two hours at a stretch at the Round Table Conference in London, for which he had not even prepared. When his secretary Mr. Desai was asked, 'How could Gandhiji speak non-stop for two hours, that too so fluently and put forth his point so firmly?', Mr. Desai replied, 'Whatever Gandhiji thinks are also his feelings, his words as well as his actions. That's why it is easy for him.'

Often, Gandhiji would wait till the last minute to make decisions. He would never declare any of his decisions as final until he got the answer from within.

Gandhiji had an amazing capability of making correct decisions.

Under his leadership, a magical wave of enthusiasm and sacrifice swept over the society. This wave started wiping out the discriminating behaviour towards untouchables from the hearts of people. The whole world was astonished thinking what miraculous power this small and skinny personality had which awakens the conscience of people time and again and creates a new awareness in them.

No man can become virtuous in a day. He needs to put in efforts for a sustained period of time to achieve this. Gandhiji worked on himself in every incident. He questioned himself in every event. That is why his name is being taken among today's honourable people.

Full of virtues such as self-confidence, intuition, decisionpower, will-power, trustworthiness, self-reliance, simplicity and ease, honest thinking, fearlessness, dedication, morality, courage, inner strength, deceit-free, etc., Gandhiji was an epitome of strong Foundation90. By adopting these qualities, we can become honourable and make our children honourable.

A Unique Combination of Love, Affection, Sacrifice and Service

Mother Teresa

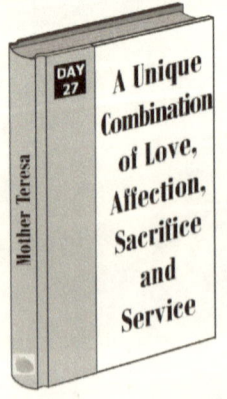

There are several people in this world who are not known by their Top10 but by their character. Their life demonstrates how to conduct extraordinarily in adverse circumstances. One name among such people is Mother Teresa, in whom one can see a unique combination of love, compassion, affection, service and sacrifice.

Today, Mother Teresa is not among Mother Teresa us but reading the books written on her life brings alive the purity of her life. Her external appearance (Top10) was extremely ordinary, but within her she had incredible selfconfidence. Her Foundation90 was as strong as the roots of a magnanimous tree. Due to this, Mother Teresa was as active in her old age as she was during her youth. The source of her energy was the undying feeling of service, due to which she remained dedicated towards her mission all her life.

Mother Teresa showered her love on the poor, helpless and disabled people like a mother towards her child. She became an idol representing God for the lepers, the old, the sick, and destitute children. Mother Teresa embraced lepers whose wounds oozed pus, over which flies would hover around, and whom the society had outcast. She served them with great devotion. Such an ocean of compassion and love would flow from her heart that even the sick would start considering themselves as healthy. No ordinary person could do this kind of work but it was easy for Mother Teresa because of her feeling of love and compassion.

Every country of this world was Mother Teresa's work area. She spread her pure love everywhere she went. Every sad being was the same in her eyes. She healed everyone with her balm of affection. Mother's affectionate touch made orphans, abandoned old people and very sick people forget all their pains and problems.

An incident had occurred in Mother's life, which inspired her to firmly resolve to fight poverty. This incident occurred around the time that Mother had just inaugurated 'Missionaries of Charity'. One day, she had gone to the Moti Jheel slum area in Calcutta. It was raining very heavily at that time. In this condition, a poor lady was standing under a roofless hut holding her child. She had been unable to pay the rent of eight rupees for that hut and so the owner has ripped off its roof. The lady's clothes, the rice, the mud oven had all become wet. Seeing this, Mother somehow arranged for eight rupees and got the hut's roof restored. This incident depicts Mother's endless compassion.

One morning, Mother found a lady unconscious on the streets. She was still breathing. Looking at her condition,

Mother took her to the nearest hospital. Despite a lot of pleading by Mother, the doctor refused to treat that lady due to unavailability of a bed. But Mother did not accept defeat. She kept waiting for five hours with the lady in her lap. Soon it was evening and the doctor emerged to leave for home. He was astounded to see Mother still waiting with the lady in her lap. Seeing her love and her commitment for selfless service, the doctor was overwhelmed and accepted his defeat. He quickly spread a mattress on the floor and started treating the sick lady. The poor lady could not survive but this incident taught a great deal to many.

After that day, whenever Mother took any destitute sick woman to the hospital, there would be no delay in beginning the treatment.

Once, to honour Mother's service and dedication, Pope John Paul presented her an expensive car as a gift. Mother stayed away from luxuries, and therefore did not wish to accept this expensive gift. But she also had a lot of reverence and respect for the Pope. Due to this she was unable to refuse his present.

Therefore she accepted the car. However, in this situation, everyone got to know Mother's practical nature. She announced an auction of the car. The auction generated five lakh rupees. She donated this money to Shantinagar Leprosy Patients Rehabilitation Scheme in Calcutta. In this way, she would utilise gifts received from India and abroad for her charity work. Mother was filled with so much love for service that greed or desire for anything was never able to tempt her. She always remained detached from everything that lured the mind and was incessantly engaged in service.

Once, Mother went to Manila, Philippines, for opening a new charitable home. The custom officials demanded tax on medicines. This brought sternness on Mother's face. She spoke in a firm tone, 'We do not take anything from the Government, and therefore, also do not owe it anything. Some other nation has donated these medicines for the sick residents of this country. Therefore, we will definitely not pay any tax.' She spoke with the country's president, Mrs. Cory Aquino, and obtained a waiver from the taxes levied on the medicines.

All these incidents bring out Mother Teresa's character before us. She is an example of a resolute Foundation90. Her life is proof that love, compassion, affection, sacrifice and service can make even your external appearance look so beautiful!

Symbol of Knowledge, Inspiration and Great Deeds

Swami Vivekananda

How does a man achieve a noble character? What qualities does he have? How does his personality influence others? This is exemplified by the life-sketch of Swami Vivekananda.

Swami Vivekananda was and will remain a source of inspiration for youth. He was a symbol of knowledge, inspiration and great deeds. He taught the youth of India Swami Vivekananda to walk on the highest path and also taught them to serve with a selfless attitude. His dream was to see a 'Fearless India, Strong India'. Hence, he had given the message: 'Cowardice and weakness are sins, which everyone must get rid of.' His birthday is celebrated in India as 'National Youth Day'.

Swami Vivekananda was such an exceptional disciple that his mention always brings the memory of his inimitable master, Ramakrishna Paramahansa. When the disciple is ready to receive the highest knowledge, the Guru has to arrive. The arrival of Ramakrishna Paramahansa into the life of Swami Vivekananda was also a great event, which is an ideal example of a Guru-disciple relationship.

Sharp Intellect of Narendra

Vivekananda (formerly known as Narendra) was a bright student. He was also a leader in his school. He had once delivered a speech in his school too. Nobody was ready to get up and go on stage to say some words about a teacher who was leaving the school. At that time, Narendra came up and spoke about that teacher. This was his first speech. Narendra had a sharp intellect. He would always think logically. He would meet all the religious missionaries who came to his city and his curiosity was so strong that he straightaway would ask them, 'Have you seen God?' Everyone who heard this question would be taken aback.

Encounter with Ramakrishna Paramahansa

After his B.A. examinations, he went to meet Ramakrishna at Dakshineshwar. This was the second incident in his life, where his life took a U-turn. He was made to sit after reaching there and also asked to sing devotional hymns *(bhajans)*.

Ramakrishna got absorbed into samadhi upon hearing Narendra's hymn. As soon as the hymn was over, he took Narendra by his hand and led him to the courtyard and told him, 'Why did you take such a long time to reach here? How could you stay away from me for so long? You do not know who you are. You are *Narayan* (God) in the form of *nar* (man).' Narendra was stunned.

Narendra also asked Ramakrishna Paramahansa, 'Have you seen God?' Ramakrishna replied, 'Yes, yes, definitely I have seen God. Just as I see you, I see him and also talk to him. If you wish, he can be shown to you too.' But these words and behaviour seemed insane to Vivekananda at first. Subsequently, Ramakrishna Paramahansa went back to his room and sat there. Narendra returned from there thinking that he had met a mad saint because Ramakrishna had left him only after taking his promise that he would return soon. After a month, he again felt like seeing Ramakrishna. He went to meet him and for the first time he experienced the state of samadhi. But he did not understand this experience at that time.

Certain rules had been made for all disciples who came to Ramakrishna. But he would say for Narendra, 'There are no rules for him. It does not matter whether he follows them or not. Rules are made for weak people; there are no rules for him.' Listening to such words, even Narendra would feel surprised.

Incidents in the life of Vivekananda

The most sorrowful incident that had occurred during that time in Narendra's life was his father's death. He felt very sad. He had to now shoulder all responsibilities of his family. They were finding it difficult to make two ends meet. He was trying to find a job, but in vain. Some of his friends refused to help him and some others were afraid to help him for fear of hurting his self-respect. They knew what type of a person Narendra was. At times, someone would indirectly tell him, 'Come over to my place to eat. We are having a party.' Narendra would refrain from going, thinking how he could go to a party when his family members were starving.

Demand of Devotion and Sacrifice

One day Narendra went to Ramakrishna Paramahansa and asked for something for the first time. He said, 'You speak with Goddess Kali every day. Please ask her something for my family so that our life becomes a bit easy.' Ramakrishna replied, 'I do not ask for such things. Why don't you go yourself and ask?' Vivekananda went to the temple and sat before Mother Kali. After some time, in his devotion he felt an amazing experience, and he returned without asking anything.

The next day Ramakrishna asked, 'Did you ask for something?' Narendra replied, 'I was not able to ask.' He said, 'Fine. Go to the temple again today.' When Narendra went for the second time to the temple, he had the same experience again. When he was sent for the third time, even then he was not able to ask anything for his family, he only asked, 'Give me devotion. Give me the power of sacrifice.' Asking for such blessings, he returned. Ramakrishna assured him, 'You will not be able to do this. Don't worry. Go home. There will never be dearth of bread or clothes in your home.' After this incident, a major transformation took place in his life. He got the job of a translator and later that of a teacher. Thus a permanent arrangement was made for bread for his family. This did not make his family as well-to-do as before, but they did not have to scavenge around for their basic requirements.

Ramakrishna would always tell his disciples about Narendra, 'Look at him! He is such a good student. He studies so well. Look at his manner of speaking. Look how sweet he sings! No one has so many virtues. He is foremost in studies and also very good at religious discussions. Such a person is rare to find.'

Vivekananda's journey

Another similar incident displays Vivekananda's inner strength, and his love and dedication for people. Every religion was represented at the World Parliament of Religions held in America. Vivekananda also went to America. He was looted of all his money before he reached the conference. He was walking on foot, when an old woman helped him reach the venue of the conference. At his first speech there, he started with the words, 'My dear brothers and sisters...' At this opening line, everybody clapped for a very long time because the people assembled there were surprised to hear words such as 'brothers and sisters', instead of 'ladies and gentlemen'. To call someone as a brother or a sister is a very big thing for people abroad.

No one in India will find anything new in this but people there found it new and wonderful. They felt, 'How could someone call everyone as brothers or sisters with so much ease? How can someone make such a close relationship with new people in a strange city?' and Vivekananda had said this with great love and ease. People appreciated this. His name and speech was published in newspapers.

While listening to his speeches, some people would also ignore him and some would spread negative things about him. These people would spread rumours in those places where Vivekananda was invited for delivering speeches. And when he reached those places, he would find them locked. Later, when their misunderstandings got cleared, these people came to him asking for forgiveness.

Teachings of Swami Vivekananda

A message which recurred in Swamiji's speeches is: 'There are only two sins in this world – one is cowardice and the other is weakness. Hence become fearless and discard those thoughts from your mind that weaken you. Strengthen your body such that your nerves become that of steel and your intellect is not filled with waste.' Due to ignorance, people fill their intellect with trash. Those, who get involved in weakening topics, get repeatedly caught in worldly illusions. Swamiji would tell people the importance of exercise for the body. If the body is strong, you can easily perform your spiritual practice *(sadhana)*. His teachings would also say, 'If you wish to attain God, and remember him, then do so in the way a woman remembers her lost husband. Only if you remember God with that intensity, can you attain him.'

Swami Vivekananda always followed his Guru's teachings. Whatever he preached, he had practised in his own life. One of his teachings was, 'It is better that the body dies by working hard, rather than living in lethargy for a thousand years.' He worked constantly. He would go to various places all the time. Karma (action or deeds) was worship for him.

From these incidents and teachings, which are described very briefly here, the pure but powerful character of Swami Vivekananda is revealed to us.

Ocean of Detachment, Devotion, Service and Forgiveness

Saint Tukaram

The life of Saint Tukaram is a beautiful amalgamation of detachment and devotion, and an ocean of compassion and forgiveness.

He has related his experiences in an easy and honest manner in the form of his *abhangas* (type of hymns), which even today people sing. Tukaram Maharaj imparted the knowledge of his experiences to people of his times. He has written his teachings in his biography, in a simple and beautiful manner, filled with devotion, in common man's language. He was an ordinary person but he became extraordinary through his divine devotion and selfless nature.

May every person of this society become good and virtuous so that an ideal society can be ushered in – these were the thoughts that frequently appeared in Tukaram's mind. He described through his *abhangas* how ego escalates in the society on the basis of colour, caste and wealth, and how it can be destroyed. He realised God through the grace of his Guru and dedicated his life for the welfare of the world.

When people in the society are not able to identify their wealth of character and when moral values of life start declining, such great saints are born into this world.

Saint Tukaram was born in a *shudra* (considered to be the lowest caste in India in those times) family. He lived his life as a *vaishya*, which involves business. He had a grocery shop, where he worked as a grocer. He defended the Truth and thereby became a *kshatriya* as well and also a *brahmin* by imparting knowledge to people. All four states (castes) assimilated in the same person – *shudra, vaishya, kshatriya* and *brahmin*.

His parents were good people who lived a truthful life. There was a temple of Panduranga inside his home. He was raised in a good environment since childhood. Thus right from the beginning, his foundation was being consolidated. His father used to go on a pilgrimage every year to Pandharpur. Thus love for God and other such qualities of his parents had been instilled in him as a child.

Beginning of responsibilities

At the age of 12-13 years, he was given the responsibility of managing their household business. He had to manage their shop because his elder brother was not bright enough and his younger brother was still very young. Thus at a very young age he came to know what is money and what is wealth. Not only this, but also he was married twice. His first marriage took place when he was 13-14 years old and second when he was 15-16. His first wife was of a very calm nature while his second wife became instrumental for him. She tormented him to no end and thus pushed him on the path of God. She was from a rich family and had a very volatile nature. Since Tukaram was doing business, it was very easy for him to give money to the poor and needy. His wife would howl over this and keep nagging him saying, 'What a useless husband I have got!'

Beginning of depressing events

Until his parents were alive, they would take care of everything. But at the age of 17, he lost his parents. His elder brother, who was married, also lost his wife. A year after that, his elder brother left the house. For some years, Tukaram worked with a lot of courage because he was facing all kinds of difficulties together. After his parents' death, he had to take care of one son, two wives, a younger brother, shop, home, cattle, lenders and borrowers. Money had been borrowed from some people as well as money had been lent to some others. He even had the responsibility to manage his business accounts. He passed a few more years bravely coping with such circumstances, but life did not stop testing him here.

The village was struck by a severe drought. Several lives were lost; he lost his respect as well as business. His way of doing business did not allow him to ask for his money back from those he had lent money to, and those he had borrowed from would always pester him for their money. Anyone could easily dupe him. When he would come home and report these happenings to his wife, she would in turn curse him. He was abused a lot, but remained silent.

Saint Tukaram has said in his *abhangas*, 'Just as in a war the warrior's strength intensifies on seeing his defeat, in the same way a devotee's reverence intensifies during testing times.' He has further said, 'He who rides over adversities, and does not let the adversities ride him over, is a true devotee.' How can someone that succumbs become a devotee? This means that we must prepare ourselves such that our foundation remains unwavering despite adversities. Our dedication to God must not diminish during trials and tribulations.

He went bankrupt at that time. Not only that, but he also lost three of his bulls. His first wife and son lost their lives because of famine and drought in the village. He did not even have enough money to feed them. This was the most heartrending event of his life.

He also lost the status and respect he had in the society. Difficulties were always there; in addition nasty people would always harass him. However, Tukaram remained unyielding and continued to work. He kept doing whatever he could. He did not have hatred or ill intent for anyone. Although people said vicious things to him, he never behaved badly with anyone.

When devotion is on the rise, a person's life takes a new turn. Tukaram's life also took a new turn. He would go and contemplate on the Bamnath hill behind the river Indrayani.

He would remain there all day. He would go in the morning and return at night. At times it also happened that he would be missing for days. His wife would then set out in search of him. She would cajole him and bring him back from the jungles and mountains. She would also abuse him later.

Saint Tukaram had seen everything at a very young age. At the age of 23, he found his Guru in his dream and attained supreme wisdom. After that, he began expressing the Supreme Truth in the form of abhangas. New abhangas would flow from him every day. This offended a lot of people. The priests and learned men of that time who considered themselves as very knowledgeable started getting upset. They began to complain about Tukaram to the village head, Shastri. However it was very clear to Tukaram that Vitthal (God) was speaking through him. He would say, 'If Vitthal is speaking, then what can I do?... If the abhangas that are emerging from my body resemble the Vedas and scriptures, what can I do?' He was not reading them from somewhere. But how can ordinary people understand this?

Beginning of service

A brahmin named Mumbaji had come to stay in his neighbourhood. He would always despise Tukaram but would also go to listen to his devotional songs. With Mumbaji as their neighbour, the people around are bound to face problems. People like Mumbaji want comfort and security more than knowledge. If he faced any inconvenience, he would condemn Tukaram saying, 'You pretend to be a big saint. Your cow chewed away my plant... ' Once he was so cross, that he beat up Tukaram with a tree branch.

This incident from his life teaches us what patience is and how one must behave with other people. When Mumbaji did not come for that evening's devotional session, Tukaram asked, 'Where is Mumbaji? Why hasn't he come?' He later went to see Mumbaji at his place and told him, 'Perhaps your hands are paining. Shall I massage your hands?' Mumbaji felt deeply ashamed thinking, 'What have I done?'

You will be able to raise the level of consciousness of another person if you have tolerance, patience, if you spend some time and contemplate, if you go onto the Zero experience, and find answers from the inner silence. Otherwise man thinks, 'If the opposite person is wrong, I have the right to punish him.'

When travellers would come to the village with luggage on their heads, Tukaram would tell them, 'Where are you going? I will carry your luggage for you.' In this way, he would render various services. During the hot summers he would fan all those who came to listen to his teachings and hymns. He never felt embarrassed in doing such type of activities. He would arrange hot water for soaking the feet for someone tired, warm his feet, prepare food for him, and make all other arrangements. He would arrange for people to stay in an inexpensive lodge *(dharamashala)* or at his own house.

The main point which features in Tukaram's teachings is 'Staying in the company of virtuous people.' When you stay in the company of virtuous people, you would automatically get rid of the five vices such as eyeing others' wealth or others' women, criticism of others, violence on others and desiring respect from others. He says, 'It's of no use to look at shade from a distance. You can feel it only by going under it.

When you go there, you will feel the coolness, and all troubles arising out of heat and anger will disappear.' This is why it is advised to be in the company of upright people. Only by being in their company, can we become upright.

His teachings are – study of scriptures and contemplation. He had himself read all the books available to him at that time. He knew that reading invokes contemplation, through contemplation one can reach the depths of Truth, depth will invoke change in actions, through such actions the present will be transformed, and a transformed present can create a golden future. A golden future will bring happiness for oneself and for all. That is why study, reading and contemplation will always remain important.

He has spoken about devotion in his teachings. Devotion must arise in every man, which means everyone should fall in love with God. He has also provided understanding to people on what is possible through devotion. He had attained his Guru and Panduranga (God) only through his power of devotion.

He has also given importance to purity of mind. Only after achieving purity of mind, our body will begin to work for us, i.e. it will support us and not hamper us in our expression of the Truth. A body full of tendencies will handicap us throughout life. We will remain stuck in some tendency or the other of the mind, due to which self-realisation will become impossible. Tukaram has also asked to focus on good qualities. He says, 'Focus on the *kasturi* (musk in the navel of the musk deer). Do not focus on its form or appearance. We have to imbibe the qualities of kasturi.' This reiterates the fact that we must pay more attention towards making our Foundation90. unwavering and not spend time unnecessarily on our Top10.

DAY 30

Let Your Guru Shape Your Foundation

Recognise the tools of the Guru

FINAL REMEDY

In order to make a person's Foundation90 resplendent, a Guru plays an important role in his life. Only the Guru is capable of giving him unbiased guidance. The Guru introduces the disciple to his virtues and vices, so that the disciple can enrich his virtues and annihilate his vices, to brighten his Foundation90.

The Guru can be metaphorically said to be an electrician. Just as the Recognise the tools of the Guru electrician illuminates our entire home, similarly the Guru illuminates the disciple's life with the light of supreme knowledge.

If you have a power problem and there is no electricity in your house, you call the electrician. When there were lights in your home and you were able to see everything, your life was smooth and happy. But when the lights went off and you could not see anything, the ease in your life was shattered. Similarly, there was a time when people were able to see the Truth easily. The Truth was working in their lives. There was always Lord Rama's regime in Ayodhya. Your body is comparable to Ayodhya. Ayodhya means a + yuddha, i.e. where there is no war. Rama's abode was in Ayodhya but when he was exiled, all joy was lost in Ayodhya. In order to restore your lost joy (light), a Guru enters your life.

The Guru comes as an electrician and sets right an individual's meter, wires and loose connection. Some time back, you were grumbling due to no lights and when suddenly you see light, you exclaim, 'Aha! Good that I called the Electricity Board.'

When the Guru arrives in your life, you learn the truth about yourself as well as about the false beliefs of the people around you. When you see people walking in the darkness of ignorance, you realise the grace that is bestowed upon you. You shall wish others also to learn the Truth. You shall wish that they too try to get illuminated, be able to listen to the Truth to find the bright light, and that an electrician (Guru) enters their lives too.

You will not like the electrician at first because he has sharp tools like the cutter, pliers, head cleaner and screw-driver. When nuts and bolts become loose, it leads to loose connection. When the nuts and bolts (intellect) get rusty due to the dampness of illusion (getting entangled in worldly affairs), then a person is not able to think well or take right decisions. Therefore, it is important to illuminate the intellect and awaken the power of discrimination (viveka). The Guru uses four tools to bolster his disciple's Foundation90 and to clean the rust from his brain. These are merely examples for the sake of understanding. Do not get stuck in the literal meaning of these words, but try to grasp the underlying truth.

1. Cleaner – To remove the rust from the intellect

A person is asked to contemplate a bit in order to remove the rust from his intellect. But he does not understand, what should he contemplate upon in his life? Which aspect of his life should he shed light on? Gradually, when his intellect is cleaned with the cleaner of understanding, all the rust on his intellect and the struggle from his life is eliminated.

2. Cutter – To cut the false beliefs of people

When a disciple's life gets illuminated with Bright knowledge (supreme knowledge of the Truth), he understands the value of a cutter. The Guru cuts through his patterns, tendencies, wrong beliefs and such unnecessary things using the cutter. The cutter is more useful for those people who are staunch. They say, 'I am a staunch Hindu… a staunch Muslim…' These words have got firmly rooted in their brain, but they have forgotten their real meaning. They have assumed a wrong meaning of the word 'staunch'. They think staunch means stern. These people refuse to see any other aspect of life. This is just like a bull with blinders which goes round and round a pole and cannot see anywhere else. It keeps circling at the same spot. It never comes to know that it is not moving ahead, but is moving around at the same spot. Similarly, a staunch person tightly holds onto his beliefs. He does not want to think in a different way at all. Such people need the cutter of the Guru's great teachings the most.

When the Guru cuts through your ignorance, you will feel a bit disturbed. Whenever you don't like or feel bad at some of the Guru's words, understand that he is using the cutter.

3. Pliers – To catch ego by its neck

When a disciple's ego is caught by its neck, understand that pliers are being used. The mind tells you to not go for listening to discourses, but you go and sit before the Guru to listen. This implies that the Guru's pliers are at work. In order to loosen the grip of worldly illusions (maya) on you, pliers are used. Venom kills venom. Iron cuts iron. To free you from illusion's grip, Guru's pliers have to be used.

4. Screw driver – To help us advance in our journey

Then, the Guru easily tightens things through the screw driver. The screw driver helps you move forward in your journey of Truth, because only if you have the light of knowledge can you move forward. Your car cannot move forward on the night of *Amavasya* (new moon) brought about by the mind. Only when there is the bright light of the highest knowledge, you can see when, where and what decisions are to be taken. Also, what should we do during the day and during the night, and how to be present in the interval of silence between day and night.

Do not be afraid of the Guru's knocks. The Guru's knocks with words and silence are only for your benefit. Therefore, adorn your character with the help of Guru's grace.

Take the support of *sadhana* (spiritual practice) to obliterate your wrong tendencies. Attain from your Guru the contemplation and silence *sadhana* as per the constitution of your body-mind mechanism. This is what has been called as true Yoga. Even as per the principles of Yoga, prevention and control of tendencies is referred to as Yoga. Purifying the mind is important for fortifying your Foundation90. This job appears difficult because of deep tendencies of the past and demands regular practise. But with proper understanding and by enhancing your capacity of self-observation, this job can be accomplished successfully. Now, your job of strengthening your Foundation90, Top10, and Hidden Zero begins. It is the best beginning project

♦ ♦ ♦

You can mail your opinion or feedback on this book to: books.feedback@tejgyan.org

About Sirshree

Sirshree's spiritual quest, which began during his childhood, led him on a journey through various schools of thought and prevalent meditation practices. His overpowering desire to attain the Truth made him relinquish his teaching profession. After a long period of contemplation on the truth of life, his spiritual quest culminated in the attainment of the ultimate truth. Since then, over the last two decades, he has dedicated his life toward elevating mass consciousness and making spiritual pursuit simple and accessible to all.

Sirshree espouses, **"All paths that lead to the truth begin differently, but culminate at the same point – understanding. Understanding is complete in itself. Listening to this understanding is enough to attain the truth."**

Sirshree has delivered more than 3000 discourses that throw light on this understanding, simplify various aspects of life and unravel missing links in spirituality. He delivers the understanding in casual contemporary language by weaving profound aspects into analogies, parables and humor that provoke one to contemplate.

To make it possible for people from all walks of life to directly experience this understanding, Sirshree has designed the *Maha Aasmani Param Gyan Shivir* – a retreat designed as a comprehensive system for imparting wisdom. This system for wisdom, which has been accredited with ISO 9001:2015 certification, has inspired thousands of seekers from all walks of life to progress on their journey of the Truth. This system makes the wisdom accessible to every human being, regardless of religion, caste, social strata, country or belief system.

Sirshree is the founder of Tej Gyan Foundation, a no-profit organization committed to raising mass consciousness with branches in India, the United States, Europe and Asia-Pacific. Sirshree's retreats have transformed the lives of thousands and his teachings have inspired various social initiatives for raising global consciousness.

His published work includes more than 150 books, some of which have been translated in more than 10 languages and published by leading publishers. Sirshree's books provide profound and practical reading on existential subjects like emotional maturity, harmony in relationships, developing self-belief, overcoming stress and anxiety, and dealing with the question of life-beyond-death, to name a few. His literature on core spirituality expounds the deeper meaning of self-realization and self-stabilization, unravelling missing links in the understanding of karma, wisdom, devotion, meditation and consciousness.

Various luminaries and celebrities like His Holiness the Dalai Lama, publishers Mr. Reid Tracy, Ms. Tami Simon and Yoga Master Dr. B. K. S. Iyengar have released Sirshree's books and lauded his work. "The Source" book series, authored by Sirshree, has sold over 10 million copies in 5 years. His book, "The Warrior's Mirror", published by Penguin, was featured in the Limca Book of Records for being released on the same day in 11 languages.

Tejgyan... The Road Ahead
What is Tejgyan?

Tejgyan is the wisdom of the existential truth, which is beyond duality. "Gyan" is a term commonly used for "knowledge". Tejgyan is the wisdom beyond knowledge and ignorance. It is understanding that arises from direct experience of the final truth. It is what sets us free from the limitations of the mind and opens us to our highest potential.

In today's world, there are people who feel disharmony and are desperately trying to achieve balance in an unpredictable life. Tejgyan helps them in harmonizing with their true nature, the Self, thereby restoring balance in all aspects of their lives.

And then, there are those who are successful, but feel a sense of emptiness within. Tejgyan provides them fulfilment and helps them to embark on a journey towards self-realization. There are others who feel lost and are seeking the meaning of life. Tejgyan helps them to realize the true purpose of human life.

All this is possible with Tejgyan due to a very simple reason. The experience of the ultimate truth (God or Pure consciousness) is always available. The direct experience of this truth is possible provided the right method is known. Tejgyan is that method, that understanding.

The understanding of Tejgyan makes it possible to lead a life of freedom from fear, worry, anger and stress. It helps in attaining physical vitality, emotional strength and stability, harmony in relationships, financial freedom and spiritual progress.

At Tej Gyan Foundation, Sirshree imparts this understanding through a System for Wisdom – a series of retreats that guides participants step by step towards realizing the true Self, being established in the experience of self-realization, and expressing its qualities. This system for wisdom has been accredited with the ISO 9001:2015 certification.

Maha Aasmani Param Gyan Shivir

"**Maha Aasmani Param Gyan Shivir**" is the flagship Self-realization retreat offered by Tej Gyan Foundation. The retreat is conducted in Hindi. The teachings of the retreat are non-denominational (secular).

This residential retreat is held for 3 to 5 days at the foundation's MaNaN Ashram amidst the glory of the mountains and the pristine beauty of nature. The Ashram is located at the outskirts of the city of Pune in India, and is well connected by air, road and rail. The retreat is also held at other centres of Tej Gyan Foundation across the world.

You can participate in this retreat to attain ageless wisdom through a unique System for Wisdom so that you can:

1. Discover "Who am I" through direct experience.
2. Learn to abide in pure consciousness while functioning in the world, allowing the qualities of consciousness like peace, love, joy, compassion, abundance and creativity to manifest.
3. Acquire simple tools to use in everyday life, which help quiet the chattering mind.
4. Get practical techniques to be in the present and connect to the source of all answers within (the inner guru).
5. Discover missing links in the practices of Meditation (*Dhyana*), Action (*Karma*), Wisdom (*Gyana*) and Devotion (*Bhakti*).
6. Understand the nature of your body-mind mechanism to attain freedom form its tendencies.
7. Learn practical methods to shift from mind-centered living to consciousness-centered living.

A Mini-retreat is also conducted, especially for teenagers (14 to 16 years of age) during summer and winter vacations.

To register for retreats, visit www.tejgyan.org,
contact (+91) 9921008060, or email mail@tejgyan.com

About Tej Gyan Foundation

Tej Gyan Foundation (TGF) was established with the mission of creating a highly evolved society through all-round development of every individual that transforms all the facets of their lives. It is a non-profit organization, founded on the teachings of Sirshree.

The Foundation has received the ISO certification (ISO 9001:2015) for its system of imparting wisdom. It has centres all across India as well as in other countries. The motto of Tej Gyan Foundation is 'Happy Thoughts'.

At the core of the philosophy of Tejgyan is the Power of Acceptance. Acceptance has profound meaning and is at the core of our Being. It is Acceptance that brings forth true love, joy and peace.

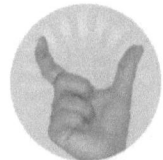

Symbol of Acceptance

The Symbol of Acceptance – shown above – is a representation of this truth. The symbol represents brackets. Whatever occurs in life falls within these brackets that signify acceptance of whatever is. Hence, this symbol forms the centerpiece of the Foundation's MaNaN Ashram.

The Foundation is creating a highly evolved society through:
- Tejgyan Programs (Retreats, YouTube Webcasts)
- Tejgyan Books and Apps
- Tejgyan Projects (Value education, Women empowerment, Peace initiatives)

The Foundation undertakes projects to elevate the level of consciousness among students, youth, women, senior citizens, teachers, doctors, leaders, professionals, corporate and Government organizations, police force, prisoners etc.

SELECT BOOKS AUTHORED BY SIRSHREE

   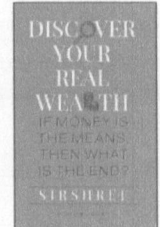

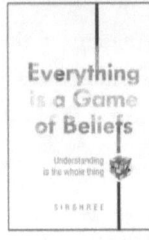   

To order these and other books authored by Sirshree
Visit **www.gethappythoughts.org**

Good News!

Maha Aasmani Param Gyan Retreat
is now conducted ONLINE in Hindi!

You can participate in the retreat from the convenience of your home. The retreat is conducted in 3 parts during weekends:

1. The Foundation Truth retreat

2. The Bright Responsibility retreat

3. The Maha Aasmani final retreat

For more details, please call: +91 9921008060, +91 9921008075

To register, visit: https://www.tejgyanglobal.org/mareg

Books can be delivered at your doorstep by registered post or courier. You can request the same through postal money order or pay by VPP. Please send the money order to either of the following two addresses:

WOW Publishings Pvt. Ltd.

1. Registered Office: S. No. 1A, Irani Market, Building No. D-38, Yerawada, Pune – 411006.

Phone No: (+91) 9011013210

You can also order your copy at the online store:

www.gethappythoughts.org

*Free Shipping plus 10% Discount on purchases above Rs. 500/-

For further details contact:

Tejgyan Global Foundation
Registered Office:

Happy Thoughts Building, Vikrant Complex, Near Tapovan Mandir, Pimpri, Pune 411017, Maharashtra, India.
Contact No: 020-27411240, 27412576
Email: mail@tejgyan.com

MaNaN Ashram:

Survey No. 43, Sanas Nagar, Nandoshi gaon, Kirkatwadi Phata, Sinhagad Road, Tal. Haveli, Dist. Pune 411024, Maharashtra, India.
Contact No: 992100 8060.

Hyderabad: 9885558100, Bangalore: 9880412588,

Delhi : 9891059875, Nashik: 9326967980, Mumbai: 9373440985

For accessing our unique 'System for Wisdom' from self-help to self-realization, please follow us on:

	Website Online Shopping/ Blog	www.tejgyan.org www.gethappythoughts.org
	Video Channel	www.youtube.com/tejgyan For Q&A videos: http://goo.gl/YA81DQ
facebook	Social networking	www.facebook.com/tejgyan
twitter	Social networking	www.twitter.com/sirshree
	Internet Radio	http://www.tejgyan.org/internetradio.aspx

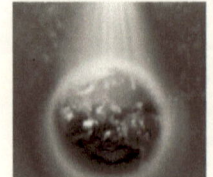

Pray for World Peace along with thousands of others every day at 09:09am and 09:09pm

Divine Light of Love, Bliss and Peace is Showering;
The Golden Light of Higher Consciousness is Rising;
All negativity on Earth is Dissolving;
Everyone is in Peace and Blissfully Shining;
O God, Gratitude for Everything!

www.ingramcontent.com/pod-product-compliance
Lightning Source LLC
LaVergne TN
LVHW040145080526
838202LV00042B/3036